AF573659

New Nutshells

Conveyancing in a Nutshell

Other Titles in the Series

Company Law
Constitutional Law
Contract
Criminal Law
Employment Law
English Legal System
Family Law
International Trade
Jurisprudence
Sale of Goods and Consumer Credit
Tort
Trusts

AUSTRALIA
The Law Book Company Ltd.
Sydney : Melbourne : Brisbane

CANADA AND U.S.A.
The Carswell Company Ltd.
Agincourt, Ontario

INDIA
N.M. Tripathi Private Ltd.
Bombay
and
Eastern Law House Private Ltd.
Calcutta
M.P.P. House
Bangalore

ISRAEL
Steimatzky's Agency Ltd.
Jerusalem : Tel Aviv : Haifa

MALAYSIA : SINGAPORE : BRUNEI
Malayan Law Journal (Pte.) Ltd.
Singapore

NEW ZEALAND
Sweet and Maxwell (N.Z.) Ltd.
Auckland

PAKISTAN
Pakistan Law House
Karachi

New Nutshells

Conveyancing in a Nutshell

Angela Tannett

London
Sweet & Maxwell
1980

Published in 1980 by
Sweet & Maxwell Ltd. of
11 New Fetter Lane, London
Photoset by
The Eastern Press Ltd.
of London and Reading
Printed in Great Britain by
J. W. Arrowsmith Ltd.
of London and Bristol

British Library Cataloguing in Publication Data
Tannett Angela
Conveyancing. — (New Nutshells).
1. Conveyancing — England
I. Title II Series
346′.42′0438 KD979

ISBN 0-421-27810-2

Series Introduction

New Nutshells present the essential facts of law. Written in clear, uncomplicated language, they explain basic principles and highlight key cases and statutes.
New Nutshells meet a dual need for students of law or related disciplines. They provide a concise introduction to the central issues surrounding a subject, preparing the reader for detailed complementary textbooks. Then, they act as indispensable revision aids.
Produced in a convenient pocketbook format, *New Nutshells* serve both as invaluable guides to the most important questions of law and as reassuring props for the anxious examination candidate.

Conveyancing details all relevant aspects of the law surrounding transfer of ownership in property, beginning with the contract, particulars and conditions of sale, and the time element. Later chapters supply the background to leaseholds, registered land and purchaser's investigation of title. Contents of the conveyance and transfer, completion, and remedies are also dealt with carefully in separate sections.

Contents

1 Introduction

Conveyancing is the transfer of the legal estate, *i.e.* the fee simple absolute in possession or the term of years absolute, from one person to another.

The diagram below shows the main steps taken in a normal conveyancing transaction. There are no differences in procedure *pre-contract* in registered and unregistered land. *Post-contract* differences exist in the deducing of title, form of transfer and passing of the legal estate.

Pre-contract

Vendor's solicitor	**Purchaser's solicitor**
(1) Sends draft contract to purchaser.	
	(2) Caveat purchaser (i) reads contract carefully; (ii) makes preliminary inquiries with vendor; (iii) inspects property; (iv) has survey; (v) makes local land charge search and inquiries; (vi) makes Parcels/Index search where unregistered land in compulsory registration area. *N.B.* L.P.A. 1969, s. 24, no need for Land Charges search.

Pre-contract

Vendor's solicitor	**Purchaser's solicitor**
(3) Answers preliminary inquiries.	
	(4) Returns one copy draft contract approved or amended.
	(5) Purchaser's signed copy sent with 10 per cent. deposit to vendor's solicitor.
(6) Vendor's signed copy sent to purchaser on receipt of purchaser's part.	

EFFECT

The vendor and purchaser are in a legally binding relationship. The vendor is qualified trustee for the purchaser. The beneficial ownership and risk passes to the Purchaser. He should insure. (*N.B.* L.P.A. 1925, s. 47, Fire Prevention (Metropolis) Act 1774.)

Post-contract

Vendor's solicitor	**Purchaser's solicitor**
(7) Vendor supplies title to purchaser. (a) Unregistered abstract (or epitome of title with copy documents) with a root at least 15 years old, tracing legal estate until it vests in vendor. (b) Registered land. (i) Copy of entries on	

Vendor's solicitor	**Purchaser's solicitor**
the register and any filed plan (ii) Authority to inspect register. (iii) Abstract and evidence on matters on which register not conclusive.	
	(8) Raises requisitions on title.
(9) Answers requisitions.	
	(10) Sends draft conveyance if unregistered, or draft transfer if registered, to vendor.
(11) Approves or amends draft conveyance or transfer.	
	(12) Engrosses deed, and has deed executed by purchaser if necessary, sends to vendor.
(13) Vendor executes conveyance or transfer.	
	(14) Searches. (i) Unregistered. Land Charge search against estate owners back to 1925 against whom a clear search does not exist. (ii) Registered. Land Registry search against title number.

Post-contract

Vendor's solicitor	Purchaser's solicitor
	(15) Lodges priority notice where applicable.
(16) Completion. Collects draft. Letter authorising release of deposit.	(16) (i) Unregistered. Checks deeds against abstract, collects deeds, conveyance. (ii) Registered. Checks Land Certificate and transfer.
	(17) Stamps conveyance or transfer.
	(18) Registered land. Lodges application for registration of transfer.

2 Contract

Formation of the contract

Contracts for the sale of land are governed by the ordinary rules of contract. In addition there must be a signed memorandum complying with the L.P.A. 1925, s. 40 (i) or a sufficient act of part performance.

Concluded contract

There must be a concluded contract. This depends on ascertaining from all the circumstances whether the parties have fulfilled the requirements of offer and acceptance (*Gibson* v. *Manchester City Council*, 1979). It is a question of construction whether the parties (a) are still negotiating, *e.g.* an agreement subject to contract, subject to survey (*Marks* v. *Board*, 1930), subject to obtaining a satisfactory mortgage (*Lee Parker* v. *Izzet* (*No.* 2), 1972) or (b) have entered into a provisional agreement which is to be superseded by a more formal agreement to be drawn up by solicitors (*Branca* v. *Cobarro*, 1947) or (c) have entered into a conditional contract. This will be valid provided the condition is sufficiently certain, *e.g.* subject to planning permission being obtained within six months.

Evidence of contract

(a) *Memorandum*

L.P.A. 1925, s. 40 (1)

"No action may be brought upon any contract for the sale or other disposition of land or any interest in land unless the agreement upon which such action is brought or some note or memorandum thereof, is in writing, and signed by the party to be charged or by some other person thereunto by him lawfully authorised."

(i) A contract for the sale of an undivided share in land (*Cooper* v. *Critchley,* 1955) has been held to come within the section in spite of the definition of land in the L.P.A. 1925, s. 205 (ix).

(ii) The contract does not have to be made only evidenced in writing. The memorandum can be made a long time after the contract. It can also be made earlier where a written contract is accepted orally. See also Buckley L.J. in *Daulia Ltd.* v. *Four Millbank Nominees Ltd.*, 1978.

(iii) If there is no memorandum the contract is not void. A vendor may forfeit any deposit paid if the purchaser defaults (*Monnickendam* v. *Leanse*, 1923). A defendant may waive section 40 (1) and if he wishes to rely on the section it must be specially pleaded.

(iv) The memorandum must contain details of the parties or means of identifying them, the property, the price or a method of ascertaining it, and any other agreed terms. A memorandum of a contract for the grant of a lease must also state the commencement and length of the term. Some terms, if not express, will be implied by law.

(v) If a stipulation which is for the benefit of one of the parties exclusively is omitted from a memorandum that party may submit to perform it (*Scott* v. *Bradley*, 1971) or waive the benefit and thus enforce the contract.

(vi) Several documents may be read together to form the memorandum. The signed document should refer to the other documents, *e.g.* a receipt would refer to a cheque but not vice versa (*Timmins* v. *Moreland Street Property Co. Ltd*, 1958).

(vii) Signature is given a liberal interpretation and would include initials and rubber stamps. Alterations in a contract should be initialled. If only one party signs the contract can only be enforced against that party.

(viii) The court may rectify a memorandum if any of the provisions of an oral agreement are omitted due to a mistake common to both parties and decree specific performance of the original agreement (*Craddock Bros. Ltd.* v. *Hunt*, 1923).

(ix) If there is an oral variation of a written memorandum, then the variation may be disregarded and the original contract will be enforceable, unless the new agreement amounts to a recission of the recorded agreement.

(x) An agent's authority need not be in writing. In *Davies* v. *Sweet*, 1962 an agent was bound even though the purchaser knew he was acting for someone else. An auctioneer is agent of the vendor both at the time of the sale and afterwards, but is agent for the purchaser only at the time of the sale (*Bell* v. *Balls*, 1897). A solicitor's authority to sign a contract can only be given to him expressly but his authority to sign a memorandum of an existing contract may be implied. A solicitor has his client's ostensible authority to exchange contracts in any manner recognised by the law including by telephone (*Domb* v. *Isoz*, 1979).

(b) *Part performance*

The L.P.A. 1925, s. 40 (2) states that the section does not affect the law relating to part performance. The purpose of the doctrine is not to allow the section to be an instrument of fraud. There must be a contract in existence which is specifically enforceable. The plaintiff must have done some act, acquiesced in by the defendant, which refers to the contract. Originally the acts of part performance had to be "unequivocally and in their own nature referable to some such agreement as that alleged" (*Maddison* v. *Alderson*, 1883). A more liberal approach was adopted in *Wakeman* v. *MacKenzie,* 1968 and since *Steadman* v. *Steadman,* 1976, when the mere payment of money and the sending of a draft transfer were held to amount to part performances, it is difficult to know what are the limitations of the doctrine.

The effect of part performance is that all the terms of the agreement are enforceable, *e.g.* part performance of an agreement to grant a lease entitles the plaintiff to an option to purchase the freehold contained in such a lease.

Formal contracts

In a normal conveyancing transaction the contract is engrossed in two parts and is not effective until they have been exchanged. The purchaser sends off his part signed and in return the vendor posts his signed part. It is unsettled, in the absence of a condition in the contract covering the position, whether exchange takes place on the posting or receipt of the second part (*Eccles* v. *Bryant and Pollock*, 1948). In that case it was suggested that because of the complexity of contracts for the sale of land it should be the receipt of the second part as the parties would then have the document with all the terms in front of them. The normal contractual rule is that the contract is formed on the posting of the acceptance.

For an effective exchange the two parts of the contract must be identical (*Harrison* v. *Battye,* 1975).

In order to achieve simultaneous exchanges in a chain of transactions solicitors now effect exchanges by telephone. This practice has been upheld in *Domb* v. *Isoz*, 1979.

An exchange of contracts is not appropriate where there is only one document (*Smith* v. *Mansi*, 1963).

Informal contracts

Informal contracts can arise where the parties decide not to bother with a formal contract, or where they have entered into a contract without realising it, or the exchange procedure falls down and one party wishes to hold the other to the contract. This is a frequent problem with rising house prices and consequent gazumping. Thus the words "subject to contract" in a solicitor's letter were subsequently waived by an unconditional offer and acceptance over the telephone (*Griffiths* v. *Young*, 1970). In *Law* v. *Jones*, 1974 it was held that it was too late to insert "subject to contract" in correspondence when there was already a concluded oral agreement and that such correspondence could constitute a valid memorandum; *cf. Tiverton Estates* v. *Wearwell Ltd.*, 1975 where it was held that "subject to contract" correspondence could not constitute a memorandum because it points away from a contract. The law cannot yet be considered to be settled; see *Daulia Ltd.* v. *Four Millbank Nominees Ltd.*, 1978.

3 Particulars of sale

The particulars describe the property sold. They must specify (i) the physical extent of the property (ii) the estate or interest in the land (iii) the benefit of the rights attaching to the land and (iv) any burdens to which the land is subject.

The basic rule is *caveat emptor*, *i.e.* the purchaser should make his own searches and inquiries and employ a surveyor to inspect the property. However, the vendor must not make a misrepresentation, must not misdescribe the property or the interest sold and he must disclose any latent defects in title. Because of this heavy duty placed on the vendor he will often try and cut down his liability by conditions in the contract. The courts construe these conditions restrictively.

Misrepresentation

This is governed by The Misrepresentation Act 1967.

A misrepresentation is a statement of fact which is untrue and induces the contract. If a statement, though true when made, subsequently becomes untrue, then it is a misrepresentation (*With* v. *O'Flanagan*, 1936).

A misrepresentation may be:

(a) fraudulent—a false representation made knowingly or without belief in its truth or recklessly.
The remedies are damages in tort for deceit, or rescission.

(b) negligent—no reasonable ground for belief in the truth of the statement. The remedies are rescission and/or damages.

(c) innocent—where a reasonable belief in the truth of

the statement can be shown. The remedy is rescission.

Under the M.A. 1967, s. 2 (2) the court has a power in cases (b) and (c) to award damages in lieu of rescission if it is equitable to do so. Rescission would not be granted where third parties have acquired rights, (*e.g.* a mortgagee), or where the parties could not be put back into their pre-contract position.

The advantages to a purchaser of suing for misrepresentation are that a misrepresentation is still actionable (a) even though the statement has become a term of the contract and (b) even if the contract has been completed. Moreover, it seems that a misrepresentation can be made by conduct and that damages will cover loss of bargain (*Watts* v. *Spence*, 1976, *cf.* damages for breach of contract which are limited by *Bain* v. *Fothergill*, 1874).

Attempts by the vendor to cut down his liability are governed by the Unfair Contract Terms Act 1977,

> "s. 8 (i) In the Misrepresentation Act 1967 the following is substituted for section 3:
>
> 3. If a contract contains a term which would exclude or restrict:
>
> (a) any liability to which a party to a contract may be subject by reason of any misrepresentation made by him before the contract was made; or
>
> (b) any remedy available to another party to the contract by reason of such a misrepresentation
>
> that term shall be of no effect except in so far as it satisfies the requirement of reasonableness as stated in section 11 (i) of the Unfair Contract Terms Act 1977; and it is for those claiming that the term satisfies that requirement to show that it does.
>
> "s. 11 (i) In relation to a contract term, the requirement of reasonableness for the purpose of . . . section 3 of the Misrepresentation Act 1967 . . . is that the term shall have been a fair and reasonable one to be included having regard to the circumstances which were, or ought reasonably to have been, known to or

in the contemplation of the parties when the contract was made."

It may be difficult for the purchaser to establish he was induced to enter into a contract by a misrepresentation. Answers to preliminary inquiries are usually very guarded, *e.g.* Inspection should show; the vendor understands so; not so far as the vendor is aware, and seldom can be said to induce the contract. Answers to requisitions are given *after* the contract has been made.

Misdescription

This is a term of the contract. An inaccurate description of the property may be of (1) the physical property or (2) the nature of the title.

The contract description of the property must tie up with the title deeds. A condition precluding the purchaser from requiring further evidence of identity than that afforded by comparing the description in the contract with that in the title deeds will not avail the vendor if there is a discrepancy.

(a) *Position of the vendor*

(i) Substantial misdescription of title or area (*Flight* v. *Booth,* 1834). The vendor would not be entitled to specific performance even with abatement of the purchase price. If there is a condition in the contract that "no misdescription shall annul the sale or entitle the purchaser to claim compensation" this will not alter the position. The only effect of the condition is to prevent the purchaser obtaining compensation if the *purchaser* brings an action for specific performance.

(ii) A slight misdescription innocently made. The vendor may get specific performance subject to an abatement. A misdescription of title does not count as a slight misdescription.

(b) *Position of the purchaser*

(i) Whether the misdescription is substantial or slight he can elect to take the property with an abatement of the purchase price. The purchaser must make his claim before completion unless the misdescription was not discoverable until after completion. He cannot claim compensation (1) if there is a condition precluding compensation and the purchaser is seeking specific performance (2) if compensation cannot be assessed, *e.g.* restrictive covenants (*Rudd* v. *Lascelles*, 1900) and (3) if he was aware of the misdescription at the date of the contract (*Castle* v. *Wilkinson*, 1870).

(ii) If the misdescription is against the vendor, *i.e.* he contracts to convey more than he intended he will not be entitled to an increase in the purchase price (*Re Lindsay and Forder's Contract*, 1895). If the misdescription is substantial the purchaser might not get specific performance if it would cause hardship to the vendor (*Manser* v. *Back*, 1848).

Non-disclosure

There is an implied term in a contract that the vendor is selling the property free from incumbrances. He is therefore liable for breach of contract if he does not disclose any latent defects in title or latent incumbrances.

He must disclose (i) any defects which affect the ownership of the property itself, *i.e.* he must have a good right to convey unless he discloses otherwise. Thus he will be liable if his title depends on adverse possession and he cannot show that the previous title has been extinguished, or where it is registered land that he only has a possessory rather than an absolute title; (ii) any restrictive covenants or easements which are not apparent. A track does not necessarily indicate a right of way; the vendor might use it for his own purposes; (iii) where the property sold is leashold any onerous or unusual covenants in the lease.

Disclosure should be by a specific clause in the contract not by sending the purchaser an abstract of title to accept before the contract is entered into.

The vendor does not have to disclose patent defects in title nor does he warrant that the premises are legally fit for the purpose (*Hill* v. *Harris*). He is not liable to disclose patent or latent physical defects though he may be liable for misrepresentation or misdescription. He may also be liable in tort (*Dutton* v. *Bognor Regis U.D.C.*, 1972) or under The Defective Premises Act 1972.

The vendor generally need not disclose any defects in title even though latent of which the purchaser knew when he entered into the contract (*Timmins* v. *Moreland Street Property Co.,* 1958). The effect of the purchaser's knowledge depends on whether the defect is (a) removable, *e.g.* a mortgage to be discharged when the purchaser can assume that the defect will be removed before completion or (b) irremovable when the purchaser's knowledge would bar him from objecting unless the contract provided expressly that a "good marketable title" would be supplied.

It used to be argued that a vendor need not disclose anything registered as a land charge under the L.C.A. 1972, The L.P.A. 1925, s. 198 provides that such registration is actual notice to all persons for all purposes. The L.P.A. 1969, s. 24 now provides that a purchaser's knowledge of a registered land charge shall be determined by his actual knowledge at the time of entering into the contract, *i.e.* registration is to be disregarded for this purpose.

A vendor will not be permitted to mislead a purchaser by concealing known defects of title behind conditions of sale. For example conditions that the purchaser shall accept the vendor's title or should not make any objection or requisition thereto will not enable a vendor, who has failed to disclose what he knows, to enforce the contract (*Becker* v. *Partridge,* 1966). Nor will the courts uphold a condition "that the purchaser shall assume as is the case" when to the knowledge of the vendor it may not be the case (*Wilson* v. *Thomas*, 1958).

The remedies for non-disclosure are rescission, or compensation if the purchaser gets substantially what he bargained for. As non-disclosure is a breach of a term of the contract which merges in the conveyance these remedies should be sought before completion.

4 Conditions of sale

The conditions state on what terms the property is sold.

Implied conditions

An open contract is an agreement to sell property at a stated price upon terms and conditions implied by the general law. The basis of all contracts is the terms implied by the general law although these terms may be modified by general or special conditions. However, these general and special conditions will not prevail over the principles of equity, *e.g.* the conditions already considered that no misdescription shall annul the sale. Further in exercising its discretionary power to grant specific performance equity will have regard to equitable principles rather than being bound by conditions of sale.

The *implied conditions* cover the vendor's obligations to convey a good title free from incumbrances, preparation of an abstract of title, production and delivery of documents and other matters which will be dealt with in the chapters concerning title.

Statutory conditions

If the contract is by correspondence the Lord Chancellor's Statutory Form of Conditions of Sale will apply (L.P.A. 1925, s. 46). The conditions are the same as those implied under an open contract with modifications, *e.g.* there is a timetable for delivery of the abstract, requisitions, and completion. Power is given to the vendor in specified circumstances to rescind and resell. Reliance on the *statutory* conditions is very rare in practice.

General conditions

An open contract favours the purchaser. Consequently vendors tend to use standard forms of contracts which modify the implied conditions. The most used standard forms are the *National Conditions of Sale* and *The Law Society's Conditions of Sale*. Some local law societies have produced their own and a new set was recently produced entitled *The Conveyancing Lawyer's Conditions*.

Inside these forms are printed the general conditions.

Special conditions

These modify or add to the general conditions and are relevant to the particular property being sold and the particular terms of the agreement expressly made by the parties.

Void conditions

The following conditions have been made void by statute:

(i) Attempts to avoid the machinery of the S.L.A. 1925 and the L.P.A. 1925 for conveying land subject to strict settlements and trusts. Thus where title can be made under those acts a provision that the purchaser shall accept title made with the concurrence of the beneficiaries is void. Similarly a condition is void which casts on the purchaser the cost of obtaining any vesting order or appointment of trustees or of getting in the legal estate (L.P.A. 1925, s. 42).

(ii) Conditions precluding objection to an insufficiency of stamps on any instrument (Stamp Act 1891, s. 117).

(iii) Conditions restricting the right of a purchaser to employ his own solicitor. A vendor can, however, stipulate a right for the vendor to furnish a form of conveyance from which the draft should be prepared, the purchaser paying a reasonable fee for the form.

(iv) Conditions excluding the purchaser's right to a copy of a power of attorney given after 1925.

(v) Conditions attempting to avoid the effect of the L.P.A. 1969, s. 24 (the purchaser's knowledge of a land charge on entering into a contract shall depend on his actual knowledge not on registration).

Some usual conditions in contracts

(a) *Vacant possession*

(i) There is an implied condition that vacant possession will be given on completion. Often, because an implied condition may in turn be rebutted by an implication, there is an express condition for vacant possession. The term means that the property is free from the occupancy, whether lawful or not, of any person, and free from rubbish, (*Cumberland Consolidated Holdings Ltd.* v. *Ireland*, 1946), and furniture (*Norwich Union Life Insurance Society* v. *Preston*, 1957). It also means that the purchaser shall have the right to use and occupy the premises (*Topfell Ltd.* v. *Galley Properties Ltd.*, 1979). By section 4 of the Matrimonial Homes Act 1967 a contract for sale of a dwelling house entered into by a vendor who contracts to give vacant possession on completion is subject to an implied term that the vendor will before completion procure the cancellation of any charge registered by the other spouse.

(ii) If the premises are requisitioned between contract and completion then the vendor cannot give vacant possession and is in breach of contract. *Cf.* where the property is subject to a compulsory purchase order then the vendor can give vacant possession and the purchaser must complete (*Hillingdon Estates Co.* v. *Stonefield Estates Ltd.*, 1952).

(iii) If a vendor fails to give vacant possession in accordance with the condition then he cannot enforce the contract and the purchaser is entitled to the return of his deposit. Alternatively, the purchaser may complete and get substantial damages (*Beard* v. *Porter*, 1948), or specific performance with abatement (*Topfell Ltd.* v. *Galley Properties Ltd.*, 1979). The condition for vacant possession can be sued on after completion; it does not merge in the conveyance (*Hisset* v. *Reading Roofing Ltd.*, 1969).

(iv) A purchaser who takes possession before completion

may be deemed to have accepted the vendor's title. This depends on the terms agreed between the parties. So as to avoid any protection awarded to tenants under the Rent Acts the standard general conditions provide that the purchaser on taking possession becomes the licensee of the vendor. The purchaser will be liable to pay interest on the balance of the purchase money.

(b) *Deposit*

(i) A term is usually included that 10 per cent. deposit should be paid on exchange of contracts. It is both a part payment of the purchase price and security for the performance of the contract. If the purchaser defaults after exchange of contracts the vendor can keep the deposit. If the vendor sues for damages the deposit will be taken into account. Under the L.P.A. 1925, s. 49 (2) the courts have a wide discretion to order the return of the deposit, see *Schindler* v. *Pigault*, 1975 where an order was made for the return of the deposit, the vendor having been indirectly responsible for the purchaser's delay in completing, and Buckley L.J. in *Universal Corporation* v. *Fiveways Properties Ltd*, 1979 who stated that the subsection, being designed to do justice between the vendor and purchaser, should be used where a repayment of the deposit would be the fairest course between the parties.

(ii) If the purchaser fails to pay a deposit provided for in the contract then there is no contract at all because of the failure of a condition precedent (*Myton Ltd.* v. *Schwab Morris*, 1974).

(iii) In the absence of express agreement, a deposit paid to a vendor's solicitor will be deemed to be paid to him as agent of the vendor. A deposit paid to auctioneers or estate agents will be deemed to be paid to them as stakeholders.

If a *pre-contract* deposit is paid to a third party either as vendor's agent or stakeholder then as the purchaser can at any time demand his money back, he must bear the loss on the default of the agent. The only exception is where the agent is given express authority to receive pre-contract deposits on behalf of the vendor (*Sorrell* v. *Finch*, 1976).

Post contract if the agent defaults the vendor must bear the loss whether he holds as vendor's agent or stakeholder. If the agent holds as stakeholder he cannot part with the money unless he receives the authority of both parties. If he holds as vendor's agent then he will not incur liability if he pays the money to the vendor who can then use it towards his own purchase.

(c) *Time*

(i) A contract should provide a date for completion. If no date is inserted the general conditions will govern the position. Normally the date fixed for completion is not of the essence. It will be where (a) it is expressly made so in the contract (b) it is impliedly so in the light of the surrounding circumstances, *e.g.* where the sale is of business premises as a going concern, or where it is a sale of wasting assets or (c) where it is a conditional contract where the date for fulfiling the condition will be (i) the date stated, or (ii) the date fixed for completion or (iii) within a reasonable time. The dates in (i) and (ii) will be of the essence.

(ii) If time is not of the essence and one party delays, the other party can at once bring an action for specific performance (*Marks* v. *Lilley*, 1959), even where the completion date has not yet arrived (*Hasham* v. *Zenab*, 1960). Alternatively after unreasonable delay the innocent party may serve a notice giving the other party a reasonable time in which to complete. If the notice is not then complied with the innocent party can treat the contract as discharged. It is arguable that it is unnecessary to wait for the delay to become unreasonable before serving such notice.

(iii) The serving of a notice to complete is usually governed by the general conditions. Thus where the *National Conditions of Sale* provided that completion should take place within 28 days of the service of a notice to complete it was considered unnecessary to decide whether such notice was reasonable or not (*Cumberland Court (Brighton) Ltd.* v. *Taylor*,

1964). Even if the notice to complete is complied with damages are obtainable for any detriment suffered by the innocent party as a consequence of the delay (*Raineri* v. *Miles*, 1980).

(iv) Although time is of the essence subsequent negotiations between the parties will amount to a waiver of the right to insist on completion on that date (*Luck* v. *White*, 1973). *Cf.* where time having been originally of the essence delay to a particular date made that second date of the essence instead (*Buckland* v. *Farmer & Moody*, 1979). Unreasonable delay, even where time is not of the essence, will discharge the contract (*Howe* v. *Smith*, 1884).

5 Effect of the contract

(1) Pre-contract

(i) The vendor and purchaser are not in a legally binding relationship. Either party is free to break off the negotiations at any time without incurring any liability. Thus if the vendor receives a higher offer from another purchaser he is entitled to enter into a new contract. The original purchaser has no redress even if he has incurred expense by employing a surveyor.

(ii) A purchaser should make sure he receives a firm offer of a mortgage before he enters into a contract. The building society will employ a surveyor to check that the property is an adequate security for the loan. The building society's surveyor owes no duty of care to the purchaser. The purchaser should employ his own surveyor who should inspect the property for physical defects. The purchaser should also inspect the property and where persons other than the vendor are in occupation of the property ascertain whether they claim any rights.

(iii) A purchaser's solicitor should make inquiries of the vendor as to, *e.g.* the position under the Town and Country Planning Acts 1947-71, details of subsisting tenancies, easements, observance of restrictive covenants. Normally standard forms are used but a purchaser should ask additional questions where appropriate which are relevant to the particular property. The vendor's solicitor should reply to these questions after confirming with the vendor that the answers are correct.

(iv) It is no longer necessary for a purchaser to make a search at the Land Charges Registry before entering into a contract. Although the L.P.A. 1925, s. 198 provides that registration is actual notice for all purposes to all persons, the L.P.A. 1969, s. 24 has the effect that the purchaser is fixed with notice at the time of the contract only of those matters of which he has notice apart from registration.

(v) The purchaser's solicitor should, however, make a search in the Register of Local Land Charges maintained by the local authority. This should reveal any orders or notices under the Town and Country Planning Acts 1947-71, Public Health Acts 1875-1936 and the Clean Air Act 1961. Any charge which is omitted from the search or has not been properly registered will bind a purchaser but he will be entitled to compensation under the Local Land Charges Act 1975, s. 10. Inquiries should also be made of the Local Authority concerning matters relating to highways, proposed development, sewers, etc.

(vi) If the property is in a compulsory registration area and is to be registered for the first time on completion a Parcels Index search should be made to ensure that there is no caution against first registration or that the property has not been already registered.

(vii) Where the purchase is of vacant land a search should be made in the Registers of Common Land and Town or Village Greens established by the Commons Registration Act 1965; see *G. & K. Ladenbau (U.K.) Ltd.* v. *Crawley & de Reya,* 1978.

(viii) The solicitor should discuss all these documents with the purchaser. He should explain to him any special conditions in the contract. It is at this stage that the contract can be amended. Once contracts are exchanged it is too late. When both solicitor and client are satisfied with the information they have received the purchaser can sign the contract and inform the vendor that he is in a position to exchange.

(2) Post-contract

The vendor and purchaser are in a legally binding relationship. Remedies are now available for breach of contract and misrepresentation.

(a) *Position of the purchaser*

The beneficial ownership passes to the purchaser who is entitled to all the capital gains in value of the property, but must bear all the losses unless they are due to the breach of the vendor's duties. Thus if the property is burnt down the purchaser is still bound to complete (*Paine* v. *Meller*, 1801). As the risk passes the purchaser should insure the property. The L.P.A. 1925, s. 47 provides that the vendor should hold any insurance monies on behalf of the purchaser but this is subject to (a) any stipulation to the contrary in the contract, (b) any requisite consent of the insurers and (c) the payment by the purchaser of the proportionate part of the premium from the date of the contract. As a last resort where buildings have been destroyed the purchaser as a person interested may require the insurance company to lay out the insurance money towards reinstating the building (Fires Prevention (Metropolis) Act 1774, s. 83). Should the insurance company pay the vendor then as the purchaser is bound to complete the vendor will have suffered no loss. Insurance being a contract of indemnity the insurance company would be entitled to recover the money.

(b) *Position of the vendor*

The vendor retains the legal estate and by the doctrine of conversion is deemed from the date of the contract to have an interest in the proceeds of sale, the purchaser being deemed to have an interest in land. The vendor is entitled to retain possession of the property. He is also entitled to any rents and profits, less outgoings, until the contractual date for completion. Any financial benefit which accrues to the vendor between contract and completion belongs to the vendor unless it is expressly included in the contract (*Re Hamilton-Snowball's Conveyance,* 1959). He must act in a trustee like manner, keeping the property in good repair, cultivating the garden and not allowing the property to be damaged (*Clarke* v. *Ramuz,* 1891). The vendor is not entitled to any indemnity for the cost of improvements or repairs he makes. The vendor should remove fittings but leave fixtures on the property.

Although the vendor is described as a trustee, he is only a qualified trustee. Besides being entitled to possession, rents and profits and not being entitled to be indemnified for expenses, his position as trustee depends on the contract being specifically enforceable. Should the contract never be completed the vendor will not be liable for breach of his duty to maintain the property.

(c) *Position of third parties*

If the purchaser registers an estate contract under the L.C.A. 1925, it will bind a purchaser of the legal estate for money or money's worth. Even if not registered if the vendor conveys the property to a third party it was held in *Lake* v. *Bayliss*, 1974, that the vendor will hold the proceeds on trust for the first purchaser.

6 Title — Unregistered Land

UNREGISTERED LAND

General points

(i) There is no absolute title to land. It is only good as long as no one comes along with a better title. A vendor under an open contract is bound to show a good holding title for the statutory period.

(ii) Technically defective titles can be forced on a purchaser. For example, where a receipt on a mortgage was dated two days after the conveyance to a purchaser the vendor was estopped by a recital in the conveyance from alleging that the mortgage was still outstanding (*Cumberland Court (Brighton) Ltd.* v. *Taylor*, 1964).

(iii) A purchaser can assume that conveyancing defects, *i.e.* those which are removable as of right by the vendor will be dealt with by the date of completion, *e.g.* that a mortgage will be discharged (*Re Daniel, Daniel* v. *Vassall*, 1917) or that another trustee will be appointed (*Hatten* v. *Russell*, 1888).

(iv) Any conditions which cut down on a vendor's obligations must not mislead in any way.

ROOT OF TITLE

On the sale of an unregistered freehold property the title must begin with a good root at least 15 years old (L.P.A. 1969, s. 23). A good root of title must "deal with or prove on the face of it without the aid of extrinsic evidence the ownership of the whole legal and equitable interest sold, contain a description by which the property can be identified and show nothing to cast any doubt on the title of the disposing parties", (*Williams on Vendor and Purchaser.*)

Thus a good root would include a conveyance on sale, a legal mortgage, a specific devise of a testator who died before 1926, a voluntary conveyance and an assent after 1925 by a personal representative conforming with section 36 of the A. of E.A. 1925. Examples of bad roots would include an equitable mortgage, a pre-1925 general devise (since 1925 wills are off the title), a subsidiary vesting deed and a lease.

Special conditions in a contract may cut down the length of title the vendor is bound to show. If the root of title in such a case is not a conveyance on sale but a voluntary conveyance then the vendor must disclose this (*Re Marsh and Earl Granville*, 1882), *i.e.* the vendor must be fair and explicit. It is unwise for a purchaser to accept a shorter title than 15 years because (i) the evidence of ownership, which anyway is relative, is less convincing, (ii) he will not be entitled to compensation under the L.P.A. 1969, s. 25 and (iii) he will be bound by equitable interests which he would have discovered had he investigated the title for the fully statutory period, *i.e.* the L.P.A. 1925, s. 44 (8) will not avail him.

PRE-ROOT

(1) Documents

By the L.P.A. 1925, s. 45 (i) the purchaser, subject to contrary agreement, is not allowed to see or make any inquiries or requisitions about pre-root documents, except:

(i) any power of attorney under which any abstracted document is executed.

(ii) any document creating or disposing of an interest, power or obligation which is not shown to have ceased or expired, and subject to which any part of the property is disposed of by an abstracted document."

Section 44 (8) provides that:

> "A purchaser shall not be deemed to be or ever to have been affected with notice of any matter or thing, of which if he had investigated the title or made enquiries in regard to matters prior to the period of commencement of title fixed by this Act, or by any other statute, or by any rule of law, he might have had notice, unless he actually makes such investigation or enquiries."

This section does not cover land charges registered under the Land Charges Act 1972.

If a purchaser does discover some pre-root defect then he is bound to take a doubtful title but he will not be bound to take a really bad title (*Re Scott and Alvarez's Contract*, 1895).

Where there is a special condition stating that the purchaser shall not object to pre-root defects the purchaser can still resist specific performance if he would be liable to instant ejection. The purchaser could, however, be sued in damages for breach of contract. The greater the defect in title the greater the damages might be as the vendor will find it correspondingly more difficult to sell the property to a fresh purchaser. A vendor who knows of a defect cannot hide behind such a condition nor can he provide that the title shall commence after a known defect.

(2) Registered land charges

Land charges are registrable against estate owners (L.C.A. 1972, s. 3 (i)). Such registration is actual notice to all the world (L.P.A. 1925, s. 198). Therefore a purchaser may be bound by a land charge registered against an estate owner before the root of title. The L.P.A. 1969, s. 25 states that if he suffers loss as a result of such registration he will be entitled to compensation provided: (i) he had no actual knowledge of the land charge (disregarding for this purpose registration), (ii) the estate owner's name did not appear in the abstract of title and (iii) he has investigated the title for at least 15 years.

The vendor has to show how the legal estate has passed from the estate owner(s) named in the root of title through various intermediate estate owners until it finally rests in the vendor himself.

(1) Documents which should be abstracted include

(a) *Leases*

Existing leases even though created before the root of title. Expired leases are generally not included but surrendered leases should be so that a purchaser can assure himself that they have been effectively surrendered.

(b) *Mortgages*

Legal mortgages and their discharge should be abstracted. Technically equitable mortgages and their discharge should appear on the title but the practice varies.

(c) *Voluntary conveyances*

Although these conveyances can be set aside under the L.P.A. 1925, ss. 172, 173, the Bankruptcy Act 1914, s. 42 and the Matrimonial Causes Act 1973 s. 37.
they will be valid in favour of a purchaser for value without notice.

(d) *Documents creating equitable interests which will not be overreached on sale*

Equitable interests arising under trusts for sale or strict settlements are generally over-reachable and need not concern the purchaser, provided he pays the capital money to at least two trustees. He will be concerned with equitable interests where he needs to be convinced that a trust for sale has ended (*e.g.* trustees convey to a beneficiary absolutely entitled under a trust), where there is a bare trust, or where a beneficiary concurs in the sale of trust property to a trustee which would otherwise be voidable (L.P.A. 1925, s. 72 (4)).

(e) *Powers of attorney*

A purchaser is entitled to a copy even if pre-root (s. 45 (i)). He must satisfy himself that the power has been exercised within its terms and has not been revoked. Section 4 of the Powers of Attorney Act 1971 provides that where a power is expressed to be irrevocable and is given by way of security, it can only be revoked by the donor with the donee's consent as long as the donee's proprietary interest lasts. The effect of section 5 is that a person X dealing with an attorney where the power has been revoked will get a good title provided he did not know of the revocation. A purchaser Y from X will get a good title provided either (a) the disposition to X was made within 12 months of the date of the power, or (b) X makes a statutory declaration before or within three months after the purchase by Y that he did not at the material time know of the revocation.

(2) Additional points on title where there is

(a) *A strict settlement*

(i) The legal estate will be vested in the tenant for life (or statutory owners where there is no tenant for life, or the tenant for life is an infant) by vesting deed or assent. It is this document which concerns the purchaser. The trust instrument is behind the curtain except in those limited cases set out in the S.L.A. 1925, s. 110 (2), the most important of which is an *inter vivos* settlement made initially by only one document. If the settlement continues on the death of the tenant for life the legal estate will vest in his special personal representatives, usually the trustees of the settlement, who will vest the legal estate in the new tenant for life. Where the settlement comes to an end the legal estate will vest in the tenant for life's ordinary personal representatives. Should the settlement be followed by a tenancy in common, either for life or in fee simple, a statutory trust for sale will arise. The effect of the S.L.A. 1925, s. 36 is that the former Settled Land Act trustees can call for the legal estate which they will hold on trust for sale to give effect to the equitable tenancy in common.

(ii) When the settlement is at an end the trustees can be called upon to execute a deed of discharge (S.L.A. 1925, s. 17). There is no need for such a deed where there is a simple assent, or conveyance not referring to the trustees of the settlement. Under the S.L.A. 1925, s. 110 (5) the purchaser must assume that the person in whom the land is thereby vested is entitled absolutely and beneficially to the land free from all the limitations of the settlement.

(b) *A trust for sale*

(i) The legal estate is vested in not more than four trustees as joint tenants. Provided a purchaser pays the capital money to at least two trustees he will not be concerned with the equitable interests (L.P.A. 1925, s. 27). A purchaser is entitled to assume that a trust for sale is still subsisting (L.P.A. 1925, s. 23) and can ignore any direction in the trust as to the postponement of the sale (section 25). If consents are required the purchaser is only concerned to see that two have been obtained (L.P.A. 1925, s. 26).

(ii) The Law of Property (Amendment) Act 1926 provides that nothing in the Law of Property Act shall affect the right of a survivor of joint tenants who is solely and beneficially entitled to deal with the legal estate as an absolute owner. However, without investigating the equitable interests a purchaser could never be sure that the equitable joint tenancy had not been severed which would mean that the right of survivorship would no longer apply. He would therefore insist that another trustee should be appointed, often unnecessarily. The Law of Property (Joint Tenants) Act 1964 remedies this situation by providing that a survivor of two or more joint tenants shall in favour of a purchaser of the legal estate be deemed to be solely and beneficially interested if either he conveys as beneficial owner or the conveyance includes a statement that he is so interested provided (1) that no memorandum of severance of the beneficial joint tenancy has been endorsed on the conveyance to the joint tenants, (2) no bankruptcy petition or receiving order has been made against any of the joint tenants, (3) it is not registered land.

(c) *Land vested in personal representatives*

(i) Since 1925 wills are kept off the title. The legal estate is vested by a grant of probate or letters of administration in the personal representatives on trust for sale. To pass the legal estate an assent must be in writing, signed by the personal representatives naming the person in whose favour it is made (A.E.A. 1925, s. 36). If the personal representatives are themselves entitled in some other capacity, *e.g.* as trustees or beneficiaries, they must, by written assent, vest the property in themselves in their new capacity (*Re Kings Will Trust*, 1964).

(ii) A purchaser when buying from personal representatives should check the probate to make sure (*inter alia*) that there are no endorsements of any previous assent or conveyance, and on completion of the purchase should insist that a memorandum of his own conveyance be endorsed. All the proving personal representatives should join in the conveyance, which will contain special recitals (see p.60) of the seisin of the deceased, date of his will and death, grant of probate or letters of administration, appointment of executors or administrators, and a statement that no previous assent or conveyance has been made. There should also be an acknowledgment for the production of the grant of probate. Although it is a document of public record, because of the possibility of endorsements, probates count as documents of title. As personal representatives only give a limited covenant for title (see p.62) they do not usually give an undertaking for safe custody of deeds.

(d) *Land vested in a charity*

(i) The Charities Act 1960 provides that consent of the Charity Commissioners is needed for the sale of land (1) forming part of the permanent endowment. (2) held by or in trust for a charity which has been or is occupied for the purpose of the charity, though a purchaser in good faith for money or money's worth will get a good title without the consent.

No consent is needed for (a) charity owned land not falling within (1) or (2) above, (b) a lease for a term ending in under 22 years not being in consideration of a fine, or (c) certain exempt charities.

(ii) By the S.L.A. 1925, s. 29 land vested in charities is deemed to be settled land, and the trustees have all the powers of a tenant for life and the Settled Land Act trustees.

(e) *Possessory title*

(i) Under an open contract a purchaser can be compelled to take a title depending on the Statute of Limitations 1939 provided that the vendor can show that the adverse possession has barred all these interests, legal and equitable, otherwise subsisting in the land, *i.e.* vendor must show full title of the person from whom the squatter took the land and prove the adverse possession.

(ii) Although most claims are barred after 12 years, there are exceptions, *e.g.* claims by the Crown, by reversioners of leases, by trustees where there are future beneficial interests (Limitation Act 1939). Purchasers should, therefore, insist on a title longer than the statutory 15 years where it depends on adverse possession.

(iii) In *Re Atkinson and Horsell's Contract*, 1912, the principle set out in (i) was extended. The vendor contracted to show title beginning with a particular document. The abstract when delivered began with the specified document, but thereafter the title depended on adverse possession. Specific performance was awarded against an unwilling purchaser. *Cf. George Wimpey & Co.* v. *Sohn*, 1967, in which a special condition provided that the vendors would produce a statutory declaration of 20 years' undisputed possession. The purchaser was not forced to accept a title based on the Limitation Act alleging adverse possession for only 12 years, *i.e.* the vendors were bound to comply strictly with the special condition.

(3) The purchaser is not bound to take title from anyone except the vendor

In *Bryant and Barningham's Contract*, 1890, the contract was made by S.L.A. trustees and the purchaser was held not bound to take a conveyance from the tenant for life. *Cf. Re Baker and Selmon's Contract* where the purchaser was bound to accept title made with the concurrence of the beneficiary who could compel the sale, it being a bare trust. A similar conclusion was reached in *Elliott* v. *Pierson*, 1948, where the vendor contracted to convey land which was vested in a limited company. The vendor as a controlling shareholder could compel the company to convey and, therefore, the purchaser could not refuse to complete. Likewise the vendor who after making a contract sold and conveyed the property to a controlled company was held to his original contract and specific performance was ordered against him and the company (*Jones* v. *Lipman*, 1962).

(4) The vendor must show title in the capacity stated in the contract

For example, if vendors contract to sell as trustees, purchasers cannot be forced to accept title from them as beneficial owners (*Green* v. *Whitehead*, 1930).

(5) Title should be shown on or before completion

Elliott v. *Pierson*, 1948. If it appears that the vendor's title is defective the purchaser can repudiate at once without waiting for the completion date. Should the vendor obtain title before the completion date and the purchaser still refuse to complete, then the vendor will be entitled to damages for breach of contract (*Price* v. *Strange*, 1978).

7 Leaseholds

Leasehold title

Under an open contract on:

(i) the grant of a lease by a freeholder the lessee is not entitled to investigate the title of the freeholder;

(ii) on the *grant* of an underlease the underlessee can call for the document creating the lease or underlease out of which it is to be derived and all assignments under which it has been held from a root at least 15 years old;

(iii) on the *sale* of a lease or underlease the assignee can call for the lease or underlease being bought and all assignments under which it has been held from a root at least 15 years old (L.P.A. 1925, s. 44 (2) (3) (4)).

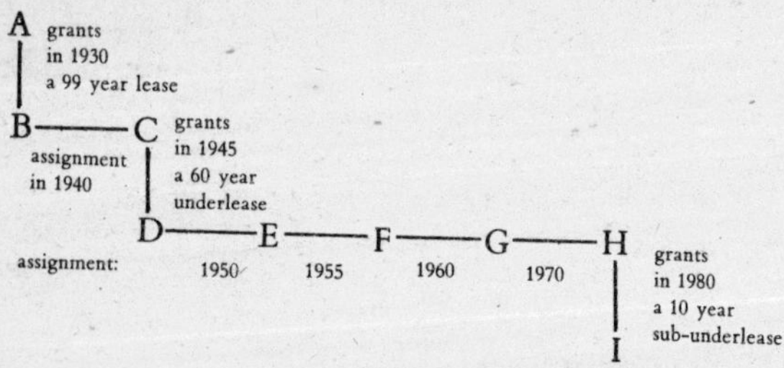

Thus in the above diagram:
B is not allowed to see A's freehold title.
C can see the lease A to B.
D can see the lease A to B, assignment B to C.
E can see underlease C to D.

I can see underlease C to D, and assignments F to G and G to H.

Put simply, a purchaser or grantee of a leasehold interest can call for the lease under which the other contracting party holds.

The L.P.A. 1925, s. 44 (5) provides that where:

> ". . . an intending lessee or assignee is not entitled to call for the title to the freehold or to a leasehold reversion, as the case may be, he shall not, where the contract is made after the commencement of this Act, be deemed to be affected with notice of any matter or thing of which, if he had contracted that such title should be furnished he might have had notice."

Thus pre-1926 restrictive covenants and equitable mortgages protected by deposit will be void against lessees. The section does not cover registered land charges which will bind a lessee even in those cases where he cannot investigate the title. Moreover, a purchaser of leaseholds is not entitled to compensation for unknown land charges registered against freehold or superior leasehold estate owners (L.P.A. 1969, s. 25). Nor is compensation available to a grantee of a lease for unknown land charges on the freehold title. The only provision for compensation is for the underlessee in respect of land charges registered against the immediately superior title. The effect of LPA 1969, s. 25, subss. (1) and (10) is that a purchaser is precluded from obtaining compensation for a land charge registered against an estate owner whose name appears on the title which the purchaser is entitled to investigate. Since the title will identify the superior lessor and lessee and all assignees within the past 15 years, it follows that compensation is only available for charges registered against assignees of the superior lease who disappeared from the title over 15 years ago. In other words compensation would only be payable where the charge had been registered against an estate owner who, pre-root, both took and disposed of an assignment of the superior lease, *e.g.* in the diagram above I would be entitled to compensation if he suffered loss from an unknown charge registered against E.

Where an intending lessee or purchaser of a leasehold interest is paying a heavy premium or taking on onerous repairing covenants he should contract to see the freehold title.

Underleases

Underleases should not be described as leases nor leases as underleases. A sub-underlease, not being a recognised conveyancing term, can be described as an underlease (*Becker* v. *Partridge*, 1966).

Where a headlease comprises more property than that contained in the underlease, and this is not obvious, a purchaser should be told before contract. Should there be a breach of covenant in respect of the rest of the property the purchaser's lease will be liable to forfeiture. For the same reason a vendor should disclose where the covenants in the headlease are more onerous than in the underlease.

Two cases illustrate the danger of an underlessee not insisting on seeing the superior title. In *Hill* v. *Harris*, 1965, the underlessee was prevented by the superior lessor from using the premises as a tobacconist in breach of a covenant contained in the headlease. The vendor in *Becker* v. *Partridge*, 1966, was liable to the purchaser for not disclosing that the consent of the head-lessor was necessary for the assignment. Although the vendor did not know this he was deemed to have constructive notice as he could have asked to see the headlease.

Breaches of covenant

L.P.A. 1925, s. 45 (2):

> "Where land sold is held by lease (other than an underlease), the purchaser shall assume, unless the contrary appears, that the lease was duly granted; and on production of the receipt for the last payment due for rent under the lease before the date of actual completion of the purchase, he shall assume, unless the contrary appears, that all the covenants and provisions of the lease have been duly performed and observed up

to the date of actual completion of the purchase."

Section 45 (3) makes a similar provision on a sale of an underlease covering both the underlease and every superior lease.

The words ". . . unless the contrary appears . . ." means that if the purchaser can show some breach of covenant the vendor will not be able to enforce the contract. If the purchaser knew before the contract of a remediable breach, *e.g.* a repairing covenant, such knowledge will not affect the position as the purchaser could assume that the vendor would comply with the covenant before completion. Pre-contract knowledge would prevent a purchaser objecting to an irremoveable defect.

The receipt is not evidence where there is a continuing breach of covenant. The lease remains forfeitable even if the landlord accepts rent right up to completion.

The general conditions usually provide that the property shall be taken in its actual state and condition. It is not then open to the purchaser to object to a breach of the lessee's repairing covenants (*Butler* v *Mountview Estates Ltd.,* 1951).

Licence to assign

A licence to assign from the landlord is usually required on the assignment of a lease. It is considered an onerous covenant which must be disclosed by the vendor. Under an open contract the licence is obtained at the vendor's expense. If he fails to obtain a licence, he has not shown a good title. Although it needs the co-operation of a third party, *i.e.* it is not something which the vendor can obtain as of right, it is deemed to be a matter of conveyance and, therefore, the vendor has until completion to perform his obligation. If the vendor fails to obtain the licence, the purchaser is entitled to the return of his deposit and his costs in investigating title. The conditions, general or special, may govern the position. Where the contract is subject to the lessor's licence being available the vendor must use his best endeavours. If he does not do so he may be liable for general damages for loss of bargain (*Day* v. *Singleton*, 1899).

8 Registered land

The idea behind registration is to replace the separate investigation of title on every purchase by a title guaranteed by the state. The purchaser inspects the register to see whether the vendor has power to sell the land and what are the more important incumbrances affecting the property. The system is meant to alter the conveyancing machinery, but not to alter the substantive law. However, it has become apparent that in many ways there are substantial differences in registered and unregistered land. In particular the legal estate is passed in unregistered land on completion, while in registered land the legal estate only vests on registration. Any defects in title are then cured by "statutory magic."

In unregistered land there are three classes of rights, (i) the estate itself, (ii) legal rights which will bind a purchaser whether he knows of them or not, (iii) equitable rights which are either (a) overreachable on a sale by trustees under a trust for sale or by a tenant for life under a strict settlement and are, therefore, no concern of the purchaser, or (b) need to be registered under the Land Charges Act 1972 in order to bind a purchaser or (c) cannot be overreached or registered but which will bind a purchaser of a legal estate with notice of them.

In registered land there are also three classes of rights, (1) the registered interest, *i.e.* the estate of which a title has been granted by the registrar, (2) overriding interests (legal or equitable) which will bind a purchaser whether he knows of them or not, (3) minor interests which will only bind a purchaser if protected by some entry on the register.

REGISTERED INTERESTS

A legal fee simple and a legal term of years can be registered with a separate title unless in the case of a lease (1) it has under 21 years to run, (2) it contains an absolute prohibition against an assignment, or (3) it is a mortgage term with a subsisting right of redemption.

COMPULSORY REGISTRATION

Various areas in the country are made subject to compulsory registration by statutory instrument. It is hoped that by 1985 all the land of England will be subject to compulsory registration. The effect of the L.R.A. 1925, s. 123 is:

(i) An application for registration of a freehold title must be made within two months of the first conveyance on sale after the area has become a compulsory registration area.

(ii) Whether or not the freehold is registered, application for registration of the leasehold title must be made within two months after: (a) the first grant of a lease for 40 years or more; or (b) the first assignment on sale of an existing lease having at least 40 years to run after the area becomes a compulsory area.

In default no legal estate will pass though it is possible for the time for application for registration to be extended.

(iii) Even in a non-compulsory area, if a freehold or leasehold title is registered and the registered proprietor grants a lease for over 21 years, the lease must be registered with a separate title in order to confer a legal estate. No time limit applies.

(iv) Voluntary registration has been suspended except in exceptional cases, *e.g.* where deeds have been destroyed or lost, or where there are building estates with more than 20 plots.

Overriding interests bind a proprietor of registered land even if he has no notice of them and even if they are not mentioned on the register. Some are legal. Some are equitable. They are set out in the L.R.A. 1925, s. 70 and include:

(i) Rights of common, public rights, profits à prendre, rights of way, rights of water and other easements not being equitable easements required to be protected by notice on the register.

(ii) Rights acquired or being acquired under the Limitation Act 1939.

After a successful "squat" on registered land the registered proprietor's title is not extinguished but is held on trust for the squatter.

(iii) Rights of every person in actual occupation of the land or in receipt of the rents and profits except where enquiry is made of such person and the rights are not disclosed.

This would include: (a) tenants and a person who goes into occupation under a mere agreement for a lease (*Woolwich Equitable Building Society* v. *Marshall*, 1952). An option to purchase the reversion granted by a lease of registered land will bind a purchaser of the reversion as an overriding interest if the lessee is in occupation even though not protected by notice or caution on the register (*Webb* v. *Pollmount*, 1966). *Cf.* unregistered land, where such an option would be void if not registered as a Class C(iv) under the Land Charges Act 1972. Rights under a licence have not been protected as overriding interests (*National Provincial Bank* v. *Ainsworth*, 1965), though the law relating to licences is by no means certain; see *Re Sharpe,* 1979, where a licensee under a constructive trust was held to have an interest in land; (b) occupation under a trust. In *Hodgson* v. *Marks,* 1971 a beneficiary under a bare trust was held to have an overriding interest as was a wife who held a beneficial half share in the matrimonial home (*Williams & Glyn Bank Ltd.* v. *Boland,* 1980).

(iv) In the case of possessory, qualified or good leasehold title all interests excepted from the effect of registration.

(v) Local land charges until protected on the register.

(vi) Leases, but not mere agreements for leases, for not more than 21 years granted at a rent without a fine.

Overriding interests may or may not appear on the register. The rules are as follows:

(i) Where at the time of first registration any easement right or privilege or benefit created by an instrument and appearing on the title adversely affects the land the Registrar shall enter a note thereof on the register (L.R.A. 1925, s. 70 (2)).

(ii) Where the existence of an overriding interest is proved to the satisfaction of the Registrar or admitted he may (subject to any prescribed exceptions) enter notice of the same or a claim thereto on the register (L.R.A. 1925, s. 70 (3)), *i.e.* it covers all overriding interests whenever created and whenever appearing.

(iii) The express creation by a registered proprietor of any interest in the land overriding or not cannot be completed at law off the register (L.R.A. 1925, ss. 19 (2), 22 (2)).

MINOR INTERESTS

Minor interests are defined by the L.R.A. 1925, s. 3 (xv). They can be divided into (i) equitable interests of beneficiaries under a settlement or trust for sale. Restrictions on the register will ensure that a purchaser pays the money to two trustees. The interests are then overreached and are no concern of the purchaser; (ii) interests which cannot be registered and are not overriding interests. If properly protected on the register they will bind a purchaser; (iii) interests which could have been protected by registered disposition but were not, *e.g.* if a registered proprietor sells or grants a long lease by ordinary deed the purchaser or lessee only acquires a minor interest which is liable to be overridden by a subsequent registered disposition for valuable consideration.

Protection of minor interests can be by:

(1) Notices

A notice ensures that the registered proprietor and anyone dealing with the land will take subject to the right protected by the notice. Rights which can be protected by notice include all matters which could be land charges under the Land Charges Act 1972 including a spouse's right to occupy a house where the other spouse is the registered proprietor. This right is specifically excluded from the category of overriding interest (Matrimonial Homes Act 1967, s. 2 (7)). A restrictive covenant protected by notice will bind a lessee even though he has no right to inspect the title of the lessor.

The Land Certificate must be produced to the Registrar before a notice can be entered on the register. Unless the land certificate is already on deposit at the Land Registry, as it is when there is a charge on the property, the co-operation of the registered proprietor is necessary.

(2) Cautions

There are two kinds of cautions: (i) a caution against first registration. Any person interested in the land may lodge a caution. The Registrar must then inform the cautioner of any application for the registration of title; (ii) a caution against dealing. This protects minor interests where the registered proprietor is unco-operative and will not lodge his Land Certificate. The Registrar must then give notice to the cautioner before any dealing with the land. In both cases the cautioner has a fixed time, usually 14 days, after receiving notice to make his objections known. If he does not object, the caution will be removed. Cautions can protect such interests as options to purchase, equitable charges and easements, but a caution is much less satisfactory than a land charge in unregistered land under the Land Charges Act both because it is subject to the warning off procedure and because the Registrar has substantial discretionary powers. He is unwilling to allow cautions to be prolonged indefinitely. Clear titles are favoured at the expense of third party rights.

(3) Inhibitions

These are orders of the court or Registrar which forbid any dealing with the property either absolutely or until a certain time or event. They are only used where there is no other way of protecting a claim, *e.g.* bankruptcy inhibition.

(4) Restrictions

These are entries made either by the registered proprietor himself or with his consent. They prevent any dealing with the land until some condition has been complied with, *e.g.* where the registered proprietor is a tenant for life there will probably be restrictions prohibiting the registration of a disposition unless (i) it is authorised by the S.L.A. and (ii) capital money is paid to at least two trustees.

LEASES UNDER 40 YEARS

The position of a lessee with a lease for under 40 years where the lessor's title is registered illustrates neatly the different interests in registered land. *Viz.*

(i) if it is a lease for over 21 years and the superior title is registered, then it is a *registrable interest* and must be registered with a separate title in order to confer the legal estate.

(ii) if the lease is for under 21 years and no premium has been paid, it is an *overriding interest* and will be protected.

(iii) if it is under 21 years and a premium has been paid then he has a *minor interest* which must be protected by a notice on the lessor's title.

(iv) alternatively if he goes into possession his rights will be protected as an *overriding interest.*

TRUSTS

The L.R.A. 1925, s. 74 provides that no dealing with a registered estate or charge is to be affected by the notice of any trust. This is sometimes referred to as the curtain principle, *i.e.* the register is the sole source of information for purchasers who are not and should not be concerned with the trusts and equities behind the curtain.

The effect of the L.R.A. 1925, ss. 20 (i), 23 (i) is that registration confers the legal estate on the transferee subject to any entries on the register and to overriding interests "but free from all other estates and entries whatsoever."

There are, however, exceptions and these appear to be growing: (i) a volunteer will take subject to the same equities as his transferors, (ii) where the registered proprietor is a trustee he will be bound by the equities of his own trust though a purchaser would take free of them, (iii) a transferee will take subject to equities which count as overriding interests as in *Hodgson* v. *Marks*, 1971 and *Williams & Glyn Bank Ltd.* v *Boland,* 1980, (iv) he will take subject to unknown entries where a clear search is given in error (*Parkash* v. *Irani Finance Ltd.*, 1970).

Moreover, following the decisions in *Peffer* v. *Rigg*, 1977, and *Orakpo* v. *Manson Investments Ltd.*, 1977, a transferee may be bound by matters not appearing on the register where he has notice either because this amounts to lack of good faith or because it gives rise to a constructive trust.

PARTS OF THE REGISTER

The register is in three parts which are kept together in The District Land Registry. A copy of the entries is given in the land certificate which is given to each registered proprietor.

(i) The *Property* register describes the registered land, refers to the general map or filed plan and contains notes of interests held for the benefit of the land, *e.g.* easements, restrictive covenants (rule 3 of the Land Registration Rules 1925).

(ii) The *Proprietorship* register gives the nature of the title (absolute, qualified possessory or good leasehold). The classification depends on the approval of the Registrar who may approach his investigation as if he were a very willing though not too rash purchaser under an open contract, *i.e.* a good holding title (L.R.A. 1925, s. 13 (*c*)), the name, address and description of the proprietor and sets out any cautions, inhibitions or restrictions affecting his right to deal with the land (Rule 6 of the Land Registration Rules 1925).

(iii) The *Charges* register contains entries relating to rights adverse to the land, mortgages, restrictive covenants and all notices protecting rights over land (Rule 7 of the Land Registration Rules 1925).

THE TYPES OF TITLE

Freehold

(a) *Absolute*

The registration of any person as first proprietor with absolute title to freehold vests in that person the legal estate subject to (i) the incumbrances and other entries appearing on the register, (ii) overriding interests, (iii) where the registered proprietor is not holding for his own benefit (*e.g.* a trustee) he holds subject to any minor interests (*e.g.* equitable interests of beneficiaries) of which he has notice (L.R.A. 1925, s. 5).

Although absolute title is the best title known to English law it is still only relative. Overriding interests are a major blot on the title and, as has been shown, it may not always be possible to keep trusts behind the curtain. Moreover, it is provided by the L.R.A. 1925, s. 82 that in certain circumstances the register may be rectified.

(b) *Possessory*

This has the same effect as absolute title except that registration does not prejudice the enforcement of any adverse interest subsisting at the date of first registration, *i.e.* no guarantee is given in respect of the prior title before the date of first registration (L.R.A. 1925, s. 6).

(c) *Qualified*

This too has the same effect as absolute title except that the property is held subject to some defect or right specified on the register, *e.g.* subject to an interest arising before a specified date or under a specified instrument as shown on the register (L.R.A. 1925, s. 7).

Leasehold

Leasehold titles can be absolute, qualified or possessory as freehold titles. Lessees will also take subject to the express and implied terms of the lease. *Absolute title* will only be registered where the freehold and any intermediate leaseholds have been registered. Absolute leasehold title is a guarantee that (i) the proprietor is owner of the lease and (ii) the lease has been validly granted (L.R.A. 1925, ss. 8, 9, 11, 12).

If the freehold and intermediate leasehold titles are not registered then only *good leasehold* title will be registered. This has the same effect as absolute title but it does not prejudice the enforcement of any interest affecting or in derogation of the title of the lessor to grant the lease, *i.e.* it does not say that the lease was validly granted (L.R.A. 1925, s. 10). Where the superior title is registered but the lessee only has good leasehold title, even though he is not entitled to inspect the register of such superior title, he will take subject to all entries which appear thereon.

Upgrading of titles

The L.R.A. 1925, s. 77 provides for the conversion from possessory, qualified or good leasehold to absolute title. If the Registrar is satisfied as to possession he is bound to convert the title (i) to absolute in the case of a freehold registered with possessory title for 15 years and (ii) to good leasehold in the case of a leasehold registered with possessory title for 10 years. The Registrar has a discretionary right to convert the title (i) to absolute or good leasehold if the land is registered with qualified, possessory or good leasehold title and is transferred for value and (ii) to absolute if the land has been registered with good leasehold title for 10 years and he is satisfied that the owners of the lease have been in possession for that long.

Rectification

Even where a proprietor has been registered with an absolute title (see the L.R.A. 1925, s. 5) the register may be rectified against him. The L.R.A. 1925, s. 82 sets out the cases when this may occur, *e.g.* to enable a person's name to be removed where the entry was made by fraud, where two or more people by mistake are registered as proprietors of the same estate, or where there are errors, omissions or mistakes and it would be just to rectify. However, by section 82 (3) the register will not be rectified against a registered proprietor in *possession* unless (i) it is to give effect to an overriding interest, or (ii) such a proprietor has caused or substantially contributed by his act, neglect or default to the fraud, mistake or omission, or (iii) the immediate disposition to him was void or (iv) for any reason it would be unjust not to rectify against him.

Contributing to the mistake includes merely lodging an application for registration, see *Re 139 Deptford High Street*, 1951 and *Claridge* v. *Tingey*, 1967. (iv) above is a vague category but it seems that if a registered proprietor stood by and allowed the true owner to spend money on the property then it might be unjust not to rectify against him.

Even where an applicant is able to bring himself within one of the exceptions to section 82 (3) and so claim rectification against a registered proprietor in possession the jurisdiction is discretionary. The court can take into account the fact that rectification would entitle the losing party to indemnity while non-rectification would not. Rectification may still be refused if the indemnity will not be adequate compensation for the loss of the land (*Epps* v. *Esso Petroleum Ltd.*, 1973).

Indemnity

The L.R.A. 1925, s. 83 gives a right to indemnity to persons suffering loss where (i) the register is rectified (ii) the register is not rectified but there is an error or omission (iii) documents lodged at the registery are lost or destroyed or there is an error in an official certificate of search (iv) rectification affects a proprietor claiming in good faith under a forged disposition.

Indemnity for non-rectification is limited to the value of the lost interest at the time when the mistake was made (s. 83 (6)(*a*)), and will generally be statute barred under the Limitation Act 1939 six years after registration (s. 83 (11)). Where the register is rectified the indemnity will be the value of the lost interest immediately before the time of rectification. *i.e.* the market value (s. 83 (6)(*b*)).

No indemnity will be paid where the applicant has caused or substantially contributed to the loss by fraud or lack of proper care. Further, there must be loss so no indemnity will be given where rectification is to give effect to an overriding interest. A purchaser takes subject to overriding interests and rectification is only recognising the existing position.

Indefeasibility of title

It is often said that under the system of registration the state guarantees the title. This is an exaggerated claim. A transferee always takes subject to overriding interests even though not mentioned on the register. The court has a wide discretion to rectify the register as may seem just, and there are a number of cases where the true owner or innocent purchaser may be left without property or compensation; see *Re Chowood's Registered Land*, 1933, *Hodgson* v. *Marks*, 1971, *Epps* v. *Esso Petroleum Co. Ltd.*, 1973.

9 The purchaser's investigation of title

UNREGISTERED LAND

(1) The abstract/copy documents of title

The vendor must deduce his title to the purchaser. The vendor does not want to hand over the deeds until he receives the purchase money: the purchaser does not want to hand over the money until he has had the opportunity of studying the title. The vendor, therefore, at his own expense, traditionally supplied the purchaser with an abstract. This gave the material contents of all documents, including endorsements. Relevant plans were attached. However, preparing an abstract is a skilled and technical job. It involves using different margins, strange abbreviations, and converting the words used in the deeds to the past and passive tense. Today it is more usual for the vendor to supply an epitome of title with copy documents attached.

The time for delivery of an abstract of title is not generally of the essence. Under an open contract the vendor must deliver the abstract within a reasonable time of the contract. The general conditions will usually cover the position.

(2) Requisitions

Having studied the abstract/copy documents, the purchaser can raise requisitions on title. The vendor is bound to answer all questions relevant to the abstracted title. He is not bound to answer general fishing enquiries, (*Re Ford and Hill,* 1875).

"Is there to the knowledge of the vendors or their solicitors any settlement deed, fact or omission or any incumbrance affecting the property not disclosed by the abstracts?"

Frequently a purchaser will ask questions concerned with the keys, discharge of a mortgage, and other practical matters. Usually a vendor will answer these questions but could reply "This question has nothing to do with the title."

Should a vendor not answer a proper requisition the purchaser could refuse to complete. The purchaser is in a less strong position should the vendor answer incorrectly. As there is already a binding contract, there can be no question of a misrepresentation inducing the contract. The vendor might be liable in tort for deceit or negligence.

The general conditions of sale provide that requisitions should be delivered within 14 days of the delivery of the abstract. If there is no such provision then requisitions should be made within a reasonable time. Time is generally specified to be of the essence for the delivery of requisitions. Where time is of the essence, out of time requisitions will not be answered unless (i) they go to the root of the title, (ii) they concern defects of conveyance, *e.g.* outstanding mortgages which are removable by a vendor as of right, (iii) they concern matters not apparent from the abstract.

There is no time limit for the vendor's answers to requisitions. The general conditions usually provide that the purchaser's observations have to be made within seven days.

Rescission

A usual general condition is that where a purchaser persists in his requisition which the vendor is unwilling or unable to comply with, then the contract can be rescinded. The purchaser will have his deposit returned but will not be entitled to conveyancing costs or compensation for loss of bargain. Equity, however, will not allow a vendor to rely on this condition where he is unreasonable in refusing to comply with the purchaser's requisition, *e.g.* the vendor must not have been reckless as in *Baines* v. *Tweddle*, 1959, where the vendor had not obtained the consent of the mortgagee to the sale. The vendor must act promptly if he wishes to rescind under such a condition and unless the contract provides otherwise, will waive his right to rescind if he attempts to negotiate with the purchaser. The vendor cannot rescind as a way of avoiding his statutory duties of getting in any outstanding legal estate (L.P.A. 1925, s. 42 (8)) or of supplying the purchaser with a copy of a power of attorney (L.P.A. 1925, s. 125 (3)).

(3) Draft conveyance

Subject to receiving satisfactory replies to his requisitions the purchaser's solicitor drafts the conveyance. This should contain an up to date description of the property. It should be sent with a copy to the vendor's solicitors for approval or amendment. An engrossed conveyance is prepared by the purchaser's solicitor and sent to the vendor's solicitor for execution by his client.

(4) Acceptance of title

It is not usual for the purchaser to examine the vendor's title deeds against the abstract before completion.

However, before this he may be taken to have accepted the title as abstracted, *i.e.* he can still object if the deeds do not accord with the abstract.

Acceptance of the abstracted title may be covered by the contract, *e.g.* the time for making requisitions and observations on replies has elapsed. Submission of a draft conveyance may be evidence of acceptance but not if it is made subject to satisfactory answers to outstanding requisitions. Should a purchaser take possession before completion then this may amount to acceptance, unless the contract provides otherwise or the purchaser makes it clear that he has not waived his right to object to title.

(5) Land charge searches

Under the Land Charges Act 1925, now replaced by the Land Charges Act 1972, registers of land charges, pending actions, writs and orders affecting land deeds of arrangement affecting land and annuities are maintained by the Registrar. Entries are made against estate owners. They enable a purchaser when investigating title to discover easily whether certain incumbrances exist and they protect an owner of such incumbrance against defeat by a purchaser of the legal estate without notice, *i.e.* the Act replaces the doctrine of notice by registration.

Land charges are divided into 5 classes. A, B, C, D, and F. The most important are class C which comprises:

(i) a puisne mortgage,
(ii) a limited owners charge,
(iii) a general equitable charge,
(iv) an estate contract.

Class D which includes (i) restrictive covenants entered into after 1925 and not made between lessor and lessee and (ii) equitable easements being "any easement, right or privilege over land." This is a vague phrase which would include informal agreements between neighbours although the parties concerned would not expect to register them. Therefore, there has been a narrow interpretation of the clause by the judges. Class F is a new charge introduced by The Matrimonial Homes Act 1967 as amended by The Matrimonial Proceedings Act 1970. This charge protects the rights of occupation of a spouse who has no legal estate in the matrimonial home. As long as the marriage lasts the non-owning spouse can register a charge which will bind third parties. This makes it possible to impede sales by the owning spouse, *e.g.* in *Wroth* v. *Tyler*, 1974, where the wife was able to protect her rights of occupation by a notice, it being registered land, unknown to her husband and after contracts were exchanged.

Generally failure to register a land charge makes it void against a purchaser of any interest in the land. Failure to register an estate contract, restrictive covenant or equitable easement makes it void against a purchaser of the *legal* estate for money or money's worth. Registration must be in the right name; see *Oak Co-operative Building Society v. Blackburn*, 1968.

A purchaser should search against the vendor and against all previous owners of the legal estate revealed by the abstract except those against whom there are earlier satisfactory official certificates of search which are produced. A purchaser who searches for the full statutory period may after completion find himself affected by a land charge that has been registered by an estate owner before the root of title. Although he will be bound by the charge if he suffers loss as a result. The L.P.A. 1969, s. 25 provides that he is entitled to compensation.

A purchaser should make an official search shortly before completion. The result is conclusive in his favour and will give him protection against a last minute registration. Thus if completion is effected within 15 working days after the date of the official certificate the purchaser is not affected by any entry made on the register after the date of the certificate and before completion unless made pursuant to a priority notice.

A priority notice meets the difficulty of registering, *e.g.* a restrictive covenant entered into on a sale in time to affect a mortgagee from a purchaser where the purchaser creates a mortgage immediately after the completion of his purchase. Notice of intention to register a contemplated charge must be given at least 15 working days before registration is to take effect. The registration must be made within 30 days of lodging such notice. Registration will then take effect as if it had been made when the charge was created.

The vendor should be asked to remove or clarify "Any adverse entries revealed by the search which are not covered by the contract."

(6) Company search

If the vendor is a company which acquired the land

before January 1, 1970, the purchaser should make a company search.

After January 1, 1970, secured charges made by companies must be registered on the Land Charges Register. (Land Charges Act 1972, s. 3 (7), L.P.A. 1969, s. 26).

2. *REGISTERED LAND*

(1) Office copy entries

Instead of an abstract of title a vendor should supply the purchaser with office copies of entries on the register and of any filed plans. It is usual for the vendor to supply these before exchange of contracts. The Law Society has recommended that the vendor should supply office copies. If the vendor supplies ordinary copies of the entries then the purchaser must verify the copies either by personal search at the Land Registry or by obtaining office copies himself, or by comparing the copies with the land certificate. The vendor must also supply an authority to inspect the register. It is a private register not open to public inspection like the Land Charges Register. If the purchaser is buying with the aid of a mortgage he will need a separate authority to inspect in favour of his mortgagee.

The vendor must also supply an abstract and evidence, which a purchaser of unregistered land could demand, on matters on which the register is not conclusive. An actual lease, even where the title is registered, will not be retained by the Land Registry. A purchaser should be concerned with its contents. Where there is a covenant in a lease against assigning without consent of the landlord there will be a special entry in the register excepting from the effect of registration the rights arising on an unlicensed assignment, otherwise the Registrar would be guaranteeing the title of the landlord.

(2) Requisitions

These will be made though they may be more limited than in unregistered land. Any overriding interests which amount to latent defects in title should have been disclosed in the contract. Requisitions should be raised on any which come to light subsequently and on any outstanding matters, *e.g.* points on possessory title, overriding interests. If the vendor is not the registered proprietor the purchaser can insist that the vendor should be so registered before completion. It is not usual to insist that personal representatives of a deceased proprietor be registered.

(3) Draft transfer

Numerous forms are available and can be simply filled in, with additions if necessary. On a sale of property the title to which is to be registered for the first time on completion either a conveyance or a transfer can be used. Where a transfer is used the purchaser, being satisfied with the replies to his requisitions, will usually suggest that the vendor treats the top copy as an engrossment.

(4) Acceptance of title

This is the same as for unregistered land.

(5) Searches

Pre-contract the same local land charges searches are made in registered and unregistered land. If the title is to be registered for the first time after completion a Parcels Index search should be made before completion to ensure that there is not a caution against first registration. After contracts are exchanged, if the title is absolute there is no need to make a land charges search against the vendor or his predecessors in title. (A mortgagee will make a Bankruptcy Only search in the Land Charges Register against the purchaser mortgagor.)

A search should be made, accompanied by the authority to inspect the Register, in the Land Registry against the title number of the property being bought. The search covers the period to date from either the issue of the office copy entries or the date of the last search or the date when the land certificate was last lodged at the Land Registry for official comparison with the register.

If any unknown adverse entries are shown by the search the purchaser should take up the matter with the vendor. If the vendor is unable to remove them, as in *Wroth* v. *Tyler*, 1974, the purchaser will not be bound to complete and may be entitled to damages.

Any entry made after the date of an official certificate of search will be postponed to the purchaser's transfer, provided the purchaser lodges his application for registration within 16 days of the date of the result of the search. The application must be in order and delivered to the appropriate district land registry. There is an extension procedure if the application cannot be lodged within the permitted time.

Unlike a land charges search a land registry search is not conclusive in favour of a purchaser. In *Parkash* v. *Irani Finance Ltd*, 1970, an official search failed to reveal the existence of a caution which has been duly lodged. The cautioner retained his priority notwithstanding the ignorance of the purchaser.

(6) Purchase from companies

It is unnecessary to make a search in the Companies Registry where the registered title is absolute (L.R.A. 1925, s. 60 (i)). Searches are sometimes made as a company might have been struck off for failing to file annual returns (Companies Act 1948, s. 353). The company's property would then vest in the Crown as *bona vacantia* and this would not appear on the registered title.

10 Contents of conveyance and transfer

"All conveyances of land or of any interest therein are void for the purpose of conveying or creating a legal estate unless made by deed" (L.P.A. 1925, s. 52 (1)). The main exceptions to the section are assents by personal representatives, which need only be in writing, and leases under three years taking effect in possession at the best rent without a fine. A Land Registry transfer, though perhaps not a conveyance, is a deed (*Chelsea and Walham Green Building Society* v. *Armstrong*, 1951). The legal estate passes on registration of the transfer.

Set out below is an outline form of conveyance and Land Registry transfer.

FORM OF CONVEYANCE

DATE … … … …	THIS CONVEYANCE is made the day of 19
PARTIES … … …	BETWEEN:
(1) … … … … …	V of in the county of , dentist hereinafter called "the Vendor") of the one part [Here insert the concurring parties, if any]
(2) … … … … …	and P and of Q of , (hereinafter called "the Purchasers") of the other part.
RECITALS … … …	WHEREAS
(1) Narrative … …	The Vendor is the estate owner in respect of the fee simple of the property hereby conveyed free from incumbrances.
(2) Introductory … …	The Vendor has agreed with the Purchasers for the sale to them of the said property for the sum of £

TESTATUM	NOW THIS DEED WITNESSETH and it is hereby agreed
THE PREMISES	
CONSIDERATION ...	that in consideration of the sum of £ now paid by the Purchasers to the Vendor
RECEIPT	(the receipt whereof the Vendor hereby acknowledges)
OPERATIVE WORDS	The Vendor AS BENEFICIAL OWNER hereby conveys unto the Purchasers
PARCELS	ALL THAT [description of the property] which [land] is more particularly delineated and coloured pink on the plan annexed hereto
EXCEPTION	except the part known as [description] and coloured blue on the said plan reserving unto the
RESERVATION	vendor a right of way over the driveway marked
HABENDUM	black on the said plan TO HOLD the same unto the Purchaser in fee simple SUBJECT TO . . .
DECLARATION OF TRUST	(a) The Purchasers shall hold the said property UPON TRUST to sell the same with power to postpone the sale thereof and shall hold the net proceeds of sale and other money applicable as capital and the net rents and profits thereof until sale upon trust for themselves as joint tenants.
	(b) [Until the expiration of eighty years from the date hereof] the trustees for the time being of this deed shall have the power to sell mortgage charge lease or otherwise dispose of all or any part of the said property with all the powers in that behalf of an absolute owner.
COVENANTS	The Purchasers hereby jointly and severally covenant with the vendor . . .
ACKNOWLEDGMENT	The Vendor hereby acknowledges the right of the Purchasers to production and delivery of copies of the documents of title which are set out in the Schedule hereto and hereby undertakes for the safe custody of such documents.
CERTIFICATE OF VALUE	It is hereby certified that the transaction hereby effected does not form part of a larger transaction or of a series of transactions in respect of which the amount or value or the aggregate amount or value of the consideration exceeds £
TESTIMONIUM	IN WITNESS WHEREOF the said parties have hereunto set their hands and seals the day and year first above written.

THE SCHEDULE ABOVE REFERRED TO
[Schedule of Documents retained by the Vendor]

SIGNED SEALED and
DELIVERED by the
said
in the presence
of

H.M. LAND REGISTRY
LAND REGISTRATION ACTS 1925 to 1971

TRANSFER OF WHOLE
(Freehold or Leasehold)

County or County Borough
Title Number
Property
Date In consideration of
pounds (£) the receipt whereof
is hereby acknowledged
I AB of as beneficial owner hereby transfer to:
CD of

the land comprised in the title above mentioned.
It is hereby certified that the transaction hereby effected does not form part of a larger transaction or series of transactions in respect of which the amount or value or aggregate amount or value of the consideration exceeds £

Signed sealed and delivered
by the said AB

In the presence of
Name
Address
Description or Occupation

Date

The date inserted in a deed is deemed to be the date of delivery. Lack of a date does not affect the validity of a deed. It is, however, important *inter alia* because (i) priority of estates and interests rank in order of creation, (ii) the

L.P.A. 1925, s. 62 (i) passes quasi-easements enjoyed with the land *at the time of the conveyance*, (iii) there are a vast number of statutory provisions (especially in Finance Acts) which only apply to instruments made before or after a certain date, (iv) time limits run from the date of the deed, *e.g.* priority period under The Land Charges Act 1972.

A Land Registry transfer is dated but the effective date for most purposes is the date of registration.

Parties

Although there are many exceptions to the general rule that a non-party cannot enforce a deed due to the restrictive interpretation of the L.P.A. 1925, s. 56 (i) in *Beswick* v. *Beswick*, 1968, all interested persons should be joined in the deed. Owners of rights which will be overreached by the conveyance should not be parties. *Cf.* a mortgagee whose mortgage is not to be discharged before the sale should be joined in the conveyance.

Recitals

(i) Narrative recitals tell the history of the title, (ii) Introductory recitals tell the purpose of the deed.

Recitals are not essential but if inserted should be accurate because recitals in a deed over 20 years old are prima facie proof of what they say (L.P.A. 1925, s. 45 (6)) and recitals of pre-root documents are deemed to be correct (L.P.A. 1925, s. 45 (1)). Moreover, a party to a deed may be estopped from denying a statement made in a recital (*Cumberland Court (Brighton) Ltd. v. Taylor,* 1964). Too revealing recitals may throw doubts upon a title (*Re Duce and Boots Cash Chemists (Southern) Ltd.'s Contract*, 1937). Where the operative part of a deed is ambiguous, clear recitals may govern the construction. It is possible that a covenant might be construed from a recital (*Aspdin* v. *Austin*, 1844). If personal representatives recite that no previous assent or conveyance has been made by them, this statement can be relied on by a purchaser provided that there is no notice of such previous disposition on the grant of probate or administration and there has not been a previous conveyance on *sale* (A.E.A. 1925, s. 36 (6)).

The Premises

These contain (a) the Testatum (NOW THIS DEED WITNESSETH), (b) the Consideration, (c) the Receipt.

Consideration

Consideration is not necessary to pass a legal estate nor will a resulting trust automatically arise (L.P.A. 1925, s. 60 (3)). If no consideration is stated the deed must be adjudicated for stamp duty. It is only where a person conveys for value that the covenants for title are implied (see p. 63)). The other effects on title of a voluntary conveyance have been discussed in Chapter 6.

Receipt

A receipt contained in a deed authorises payment to a solicitor (L.P.A. 1925, s. 69) and is a sufficient discharge for the person paying the money, (L.P.A. 1925, s. 67)). A receipt is sufficient evidence of payment in favour of a subsequent purchaser who has no notice that the money was not paid (L.P.A. 1925, s. 68)). An unpaid vendor will either retain the deeds, in which case a purchaser will have notice, or, where the deeds are not retained, register a general equitable charge. If the charge is registered it will bind a purchaser, if not the purchaser will take free whether or not a receipt is contained in the deed.

In registered land a purchaser does not see previous transfers and so does not rely on a receipt. The reference in the register to the price paid has been held not to be a receipt (*London and Cheshire Insurance Co. Ltd.* v. *Laplagrene Property Co. Ltd.*, 1971)

Operative words

Covenants for title

By the use of the words "beneficial owner" four covenants are implied in the conveyance for valuable consideration (which in this context includes marriage) (L.P.A. 1925, s. 76 (1) and Schedule II).

(i) that the grantor has full power to convey;

(ii) that the grantee shall have quiet enjoyment;

(iii) that the grantee shall receive the property free from incumbrances;

(iv) that the vendor will do any act reasonably required to perfect the title—further assurance.

In addition, where the property is leasehold

(v) that the lease is valid and subsisting

(vi) that the rent and covenants of the lease have been paid, observed and performed.

Qualified

The benefit of the implied covenants runs with the land. The only person who can be sued for damages for breach of covenant is the covenantor. The obligation does not pass to the successors in title. The covenantor's liability in damages is not absolute. He is only liable for the acts and omissions of:

(i) himself,

(ii) anyone through whom he derived title otherwise than by purchase for value (money or money's worth, not marriage),

(iii) anyone conveying by the covenantor's direction or "claiming by, through or under" either the covenantor or the person through whom he derives title otherwise than by purchase for value,

(iv) any person claiming in trust for the vendor.

When a mortgagor conveys as beneficial owner the covenants are absolute.

When a settlor conveys property he should convey as settlor. The only covenant he gives is for further assurance which covers himself and those subsequently deriving title under him. Where a person conveys as trustee, mortgagee or under an order of the court, he only covenants that he himself has not incumbered the property.

Registered land

If the title is possessory or qualified then covenants may give protection against rights and interests subsisting before and excepted from registration. There is some doubt whether covenants for title apply where the title is absolute. Rules 76 and 77 of the Land Registration Rules clearly envisage that covenants must be relevant. If they apply they would only cover overriding interests undisclosed to the purchaser. The purchaser would take subject to such interests but would be entitled to indemnity from the vendor.

Covenants for title are unsatisfactory

For example, (i) they will not be implied if the appropriate words, *e.g.* "beneficial owner," "settlor" are omitted.

(ii) They are often specifically modified by the conditions of sale, see *Butler* v. *Mountview Estates*, 1951. But where the position is not covered by the contract the purchaser can sue even though he knew of the incumbrance (*Page* v. *Midland Railway Co*, 1894).

(iii) The conveyance must be for value.

(iv) The covenants are only implied as far as the subject matter expressed to be conveyed. Therefore, no action will lie on the covenants where the vendor conveys "only such title as he has" or where he conveys as beneficial owner but is really trustee. If no words of limitation are present then nothing is expressed to be conveyed and the covenants are not implied.

(v) The covenants are qualified. The incumbrance may have been imposed by someone for whom the vendor is not liable. The previous covenantors may have died or only given limited covenants or the defect may have arisen by Act of Parliament.

(vi) The burden of proof to show who is liable for the covenant rests on the plaintiff (*Stoney* v. *Eastbourne R.D.C.*, 1927).

(vii) The right of action may be barred by the Limitation Act 1939.

Worlds of grant

Any appropriate word can be used to convey land (L.P.A. 1925, s. 51)). Transfer is the usual verb in registered land.

Parcels

These should contain a complete and accurate description of the property and be sufficiently identified with the description in the title deeds. Plans can be used and should be referred to expressly in the conveyance unless the verbal description is not clear and the plan physically forms part of the conveyance. Although the purchaser has a choice of form it has been doubted whether a purchaser can insist on a plan where the verbal description is sufficient as the vendor would have to pay a surveyor to check it (*Re Sharman and Meade's Contract*, 1936). The phrase "more particularly described in" indicates that the plan should prevail, while "for purposes of identification only" shows that the verbal description should prevail; see *Wigginton & Milner Ltd.* v. *Winster Engineering Ltd.*, 1978. The courts reconcile descriptions where possible (*Truckell* v. *Stock,* 1957).

Presumptions

These only apply where the position is not made clear by the parties or by reference to Ordnance Survey maps.

(a) *Roads*

The owner of land adjoining a highway is presumed to be the owner of the soil of one half of the road.

(b) *Rivers*

The riparian owner is entitled to the bed of one half of the river unless it is tidal, when it belongs to the Crown or its grantee.

(c) *Hedge and ditch*

It is assumed that a man digs the ditch at the edge of his boundary, throwing the earth over his shoulder on which a hedge is planted. Thus the ditch is the boundary.

Registered land

In a transfer of whole the property is described as "The land comprised in the title above referred to." This refers to the description in the property register, which refers to the general map or filed plan kept at the Land Registry. There is nothing conclusive about such plans. In *Lee* v. *Barrey*, 1963, a plan on an earlier transfer prevailed over a Land Registry plan. Rule 285 of the Land Registration Rules provides that the Registrar shall decide any conflict between verbal particulars and the filed plan or general map. According to section 76 of the Land Registration Act "the filed plan, if any, or general map shall be used for assisting the identification of the land." Any dispute will be settled by the courts in the usual way as in unregistered conveyancing.

In a transfer of part a plan is essential. The property is described as "the land shown edged red on the accompanying plan (and known as) being part of the land comprised in the title above referred to."

Exceptions, reservations and re-grants

An exception excepts part of the land from the grant. Reservations today are strictly only rents reserved though the word is used to cover re-grants. Re-grants are easements and profits à prendre. Exceptions and proper reservations, being for the benefit of the vendor are construed in favour of the purchaser. Re-grants are construed against the purchaser (*St. Edmundsbury and Ipswich*

Dioceasan Board of Finance v. *Clark* (*No.* 2), 1975). It is no longer necessary for the purchaser to execute the deed where there is a re-grant (L.P.A. 1925, s. 65 (1)).

On the sale of part of the vendor's property the purchaser is entitled to continuous and apparent easements over the property retained by the vendor which are necessary to the purchaser's part (*Wheeldon* v. *Burrows*, 1879). No similar reservation is implied in favour of a vendor except for a way of necessity.

Under the L.P.A. 1925, s. 62 certain rights, including easements which are not continuous or reasonably necessary for the enjoyment of the property, will pass automatically on a conveyance of the land. Should a vendor wish to exclude the effect of this "general word" section he should insert a special provision in the contract. General words apply in dispositions of registered land (Land Registration Acts, 1925s. 19 (3), 20 (1), r. 251, Land Registration Rules).

The all estates clause

Section 63 of the L.P.A. 1925 operates to pass to the grantee every estate or interest held by the grantor in the land although not expressly mentioned in the conveyance, or not vested in him in the capacity in which he is made a party to the deed, see *Re Stirrups Contract*, 1961.

Habendum

To hold unto the purchaser in fee simple. The words "fee simple" are words of limitation which determine the quantum of the estate. If they are omitted, the L.P.A. 1925, s. 60 will pass the fee simple "or other the whole interest which the grantor has power to convey in such land." It is unwise to rely on section 60 as (a) it is subject to a contrary intention, and (b) covenants for title will not be implied. If there are any existing exceptions and reservations made in an earlier deed they are referred to in the habendum with the introductory words "subject to . . ."

The habendum can vary, explain or extend words of limitation in the premises provided it does not cut down or abridge the estate expressly granted by the premises. The habendum cannot vary the parcels clause nor alter the grantee named in the premises.

There is no habendum in registered land.

Declaration of trust

Although property conveyed to co-owners will be held by them on a statutory trust for sale an express trust is often declared. This is an advantage if there are subsequent matrimonial proceedings. The trustees may declare themselves to have the powers of absolute owners. This keeps the equities off the title should the trustees cease to be beneficial owners. It also means that they are not subject to the limitations imposed on trustees, *e.g.* to grant leases for a maximum of 50 years only, and to obtain a mortgage for improvements but not for raising the purchase price. Section 8 of the Perpetuities and Accumulations Act 1964 would seem to make it unnecessary to limit these extra powers to the perpetuity period.

Although in registered land joint owners, in the absence of any restriction, can deal with the land as absolute owners, the declaration is still desirable in order to protect trustees who are not beneficiaries.

Covenants

Any covenants entered into by the parties will follow next. Only restrictive covenants will bind subsequent owners (see *Land Law,* New Nutshell, p.74). On the sale of freehold flats complex conveyancing devices have to be employed to enable positive covenants to be enforced against successors in title and between the flat owners *inter se*, *e.g.* management schemes, trusts, rent charges, reliance on the principle in *Halsall* v. *Brizell*, 1975.

Acknowledgment and undertaking

The vendor should hand over all title deeds on completion except where he retains any land to which they relate, or the documents consist of a trust instrument, deed of appointment, or deed of discharge of a still subsisting trust. In these circumstances he should give a statutory acknowledgment. Under the L.P.A. 1925, s. 64 he should provide copies and produce the deeds at all reasonable times for the purpose of inspection and of comparison with the abstract or copies, the expense of production to be borne by the person requesting the same. The vendor by his undertaking for safe custody binds himself to keep the documents whole, uncancelled and undefaced unless prevented from doing so by fire or other inevitable accident. Usually where vendors convey as trustees, personal representatives or mortgagees, *i.e.* in a fiduciary capacity, they will not give an undertaking for safe custody. If the mortgagee retains the deeds the vendor should covenant for production and safe custody to operate when he recovers possession of the documents.

The burden of the covenant runs with the possessor of the deeds. Once he has parted with them he is no longer liable. The benefit of the covenant passes to the successors in title of the covenantee.

In registered land an acknowledgment and undertaking is appropriate for pre-registration documents where the title is possessory, and for the lease where part of land comprised in a leasehold title is transferred.

Certificate of value

If the consideration does not exceed a specified amount and the instrument is so certified, no stamp duty is payable, or it is payable at a reduced rate. The wording of the certificate prevents the evasion of duty by dividing up a transaction.

Testimonium

The deed should be signed, sealed and delivered. It seems that a rubber stamp with a facsimile signature will be sufficient (*Goodman* v. *Eban*, 1954). On the transfer of part, in registered land, the plan must be signed by the transferor and by or on behalf of the transferee. Unless the deed is sealed a conveyance of land is void at law (L.P.A. 1925, s. 52 (1)), though slight evidence of sealing is acceptable (*First National Securities Ltd.* v. *Jones*, 1978). Delivery is some act indicating that the maker of the deed intends to be bound, *e.g.* by putting his finger on the seal and saying "I deliver this as my act and deed." Sealing by a company imports delivery (L.P.A. 1925, s. 74 (1)).

A deed delivered in escrow means that the deed is only to be effective on the performance of certain conditions. The condition of the delivery must be beyond the control of the maker of the deed. Once he has delivered the deed he is committed. Even his death will not prevent the operation of the deed. A deed cannot be made conditional on death. If it were it would be a will and have to be executed as such. A condition cannot be against public policy or purpose of a statute, *e.g.* a deed of surrender of a lease executed by the tenant which would come into operation should he fail to perform his covenants (*Plymouth Corporation* v. *Harvey*, 1971). The condition must be performed within a reasonable time (*Glessing* v. *Green*, 1975). The deed is dated retrospectively from the date of the conditional delivery not the date of fulfilment of the condition. Thus if the vendor is an infant at the time of the escrow he will not be bound if he comes of age before the condition is fulfilled. But a vendor who obtains the legal estate between the conditional delivery and the fulfilment of the condition will be bound on the principle of feeding the estoppel (*Church of England Building Society* v. *Piskor*, 1954). In registered land escrows cannot operate retrospectively as the legal estate does not pass until the new proprietor is registered.

Attestation

Except where required by statute, *e.g.* The Wills Act 1837, attestation is unnecessary but it is usual as it provides evidence of execution. In a transfer of registered land there is specific provision for the signature of a witness.

11 Completion

Completion

Completion occurs when the purchaser pays the purchase price in return for the delivery of the conveyance or transfer. This normally takes place at the offices of the vendor or his mortgagee, though it is possible to complete by post.

(a) *The task of the vendor:*

(i) The vendor's solicitor has to receive the purchase money, either in the form of a draft or in cash. He should not accept a cheque without his client's authority as, if it bounces, he would be liable for the loss (*Blumberg* v. *Life Interests and Reversionary Securities Corporation*, 1897). If the deposit has been paid to a third party, *e.g.* estate agent as stakeholder, he will need a letter from the purchaser authorising such deposit to be released.

(ii) The vendor must produce the deeds for inspection by the purchaser. If any deeds are retained, including probates, a memorandum of the conveyance to the purchaser should be endorsed on the deeds. The vendor should hand over to the purchaser the conveyance to him and the title deeds as listed on a schedule, a copy of which, signed by the purchaser, should be retained by the vendor. If the title is registered then the vendor should give the purchaser the transfer to him and the Land Certificate. There may also be other relevant documents a vendor should hand over, *e.g.* a licence to assign, lease, National House Building Council Certificate.

(iii) Where there is a mortgage to be discharged completion will generally take place at the mortgagee's solicitor's offices. A draft will be paid to the mortgagee and a second draft for the balance of the purchase price to the vendor. The mortgagee will have the deeds and hand them to the purchaser, including a deed of discharge or vacating receipt on the mortgage. In the case of a Building Society an undertaking is usually given to discharge the mortgage and forward it to the purchaser within a certain number of days.

(iv) Shortly before completion the vendors will have sent a completion statement to the purchaser setting out the monies due including any apportionments of general and water rates and rent where applicable. Receipts must be produced by the vendor to evidence that payments have been made to the dates set out on the completion statement.

(v) There may be miscellaneous matters for the vendor to attend to, *e.g.* an authority to an agent to release the keys to the purchaser, or to tenants to pay future rent to the new landlord. If there are any outstanding matters the vendor's solicitor may give undertakings to attend to them.

(b) *The task of the purchaser*

(i) The purchaser should examine the title deeds against the abstract already supplied to him. Under an open contract the expense of producing the deeds for examination and for handing over lies with the vendor. If, however, the vendor has to produce deeds, which are not to be handed over on completion, and are not in the vendor's possession or that of his mortgagee or trustee, then the expense is borne by the purchaser (L.P.A. 1925, s. 45 (4) (*a*)).

A purchaser should examine the deeds:

> "to ascertain, first, that what has been abstracted is correctly abstracted; secondly, that what is omitted is clearly immaterial; thirdly, that all the documents are perfect as respects execution, attestation, endorsed receipts, registration, stamps, etc., and fourthly, that there are no endorsed notices nor any circumstances attending the mode of execution or attestation, etc.,

which are calculated to excite suspicion." (*Williams on Vendor and Purchaser.*)

Deeds generally do not need to be attested except where required by statute, *e.g.* The Wills Act. Evidence of due execution can be asked for but deeds over 20 years old from proper custody prove themselves. Where documents are missing a vendor can produce and a purchaser must accept secondary evidence.
Execution of missing documents has to be proved not presumed.

When an abstract has been examined it should be marked, *e.g.* "Examined with the original by X and Co. at the offices of   on 10th Jan. 19   ".

The purchaser should collect the deeds which are to be handed over and, in cases where the deeds are retained by the vendor, make sure that an endorsement is made noting the conveyance to the purchaser. He should take up the conveyance or, where the title is registered, the Land Certificate and transfer. He must make sure that any outstanding mortgages are vacated or get an undertaking for their discharge.

(ii) He should pay to the vendor the balance of the purchase price and any other monies due. If the deposit is held by a third party as stakeholder, he will need to hand over a release of deposit. Where the purchaser is buying the house with a mortgage the mortgagee will provide a draft for part of the completion monies. In return the mortgagee will collect the deeds, the conveyance or transfer, and a mortgage deed signed by the purchaser.

(iii) The purchaser should inspect the receipts for general and water rates, and rent where appropriate, to ensure that the payments tie up with the figures given in the completion statement.

(iv) He should check up on any miscellaneous matters, *e.g.* keys, licences to assign. If there is anything outstanding he should obtain the vendor's solicitor's undertaking to attend to it.

The above is a very simple outline of the procedure on

completion. Where companies, new houses, leases, etc., are concerned there are additional matters which must be dealt with by both vendor and purchaser.

Post completion

(i) The purchaser, or the mortgagee, must attend to the stamping of the conveyance or transfer. Even if no *ad valorem* stamp duty is payable the document must be marked under the Finance Act 1931. An instrument which is not duly stamped is not admissible in evidence (Stamp Act 1891, s. 14 (4)).

(ii) In unregistered land the legal estate passes to the purchaser on delivery of the deed which will normally be deemed to be at completion. In registered land the legal estate only passes on registration of the new proprietor. The purchaser should lodge his application for registration of the transfer within the priority period given him by his search certificate. If this is not possible, an extension procedure is available. Moreover, where a transfer has to be adjudicated for stamp duty the documents can be lodged at the Land Registry with a request that the transfer should be returned. Priority is thus retained and the transfer can be re-lodged at the Land Registry after stamping.

12 Remedies

1. *BETWEEN THE PARTIES*

(1) Pre-contract

As has already been stressed, before there is a contract there is no legal relationship between the parties and thus no remedies available to either party.

(2) Post-contract

(a) *Rescission*

This has three possible meanings, see *Buckland* v. *Farmer & Moody*, 1979: (i) the court treats the contract as if it never existed, (ii) one party fails to perform a fundamental term, *e.g.* where there has been mistake, fraud or lack of consent, which the other party accepts as a repudiation of the contract, or (iii) the contract itself provides that in certain circumstances the contract may be rescinded, *e.g.* persistence by the purchaser in a requisition, failure to obtain a licence to assign.

In the case of rescission *ab initio* ((i) above) there can be no damages for loss of bargain. Each party has to be put back into his pre-contract position—*restitutio in integrum.* Indemnity, *e.g.* expenses incurred in investigating or proving title, can be claimed by the innocent party (*Newbigging* v. *Adam,* 1886). The deposit should normally be returned.

(b) *Damages*

While rescission in the strict sense treats the contract as if it had never been made, damages attempt to put the injured party in the same position as if the contract had been performed. Normally assessment is at the date of the breach, but in *Johnson* v. *Agnew*, 1979, Lord Wilberforce said there was no absolute rule. The date for assessment should be the date which would be most just in all the circumstances.

The amount of the damages is for the loss reasonably foreseeable (*Hadley* v. *Baxendale*, 1854). Thus a vendor is entitled to the excess of the contract price over the market price of the property and any expenses incurred by him in a resale (*Laird* v. *Pim*, 1841). A purchaser is entitled to the difference between the contract price and the higher market value at the date of the breach or when the damages are assessed. He cannot claim his conveyancing costs as he would have incurred them anyway (*Day* v. *Singleton*, 1899). If there is no difference between the contract price and the market price, the purchaser can claim his conveyancing costs as well as the return of the deposit, and any other expenditure incurred under the contract which was in contemplation of the parties but excluding improvements to the property (*Lloyd* v. *Stanbury*, 1971).

Under the rule in *Bain* v. *Fothergill*, 1874 if the vendor is unable to complete the contract because of a defect in title, then the purchaser is only entitled to (i) the return of the deposit with interest, (ii) his conveyancing costs, and (iii) interest on the balance of the purchase money if it has been lying idle to the knowledge of the vendor. The rule applies even if the vendor knew of the defect but will not avail him where he has not used his best endeavours to perform the contract, *e.g.* *Day* v. *Singleton*, 1899—failure to obtain a licence to assign; *Re Daniel, Daniel* v. *Vassall*, 1917—failure to redeem a mortgage; *Malhotra* v. *Choudhury*, 1978—failure to seek the co-operation of a joint-tenant. Nor does it apply to a spouse's right of occupation under The Matrimonial Homes Act 1967 (*Wroth* v. *Tyler*, 1974); or an action under The Misrepresentation Act 1967 (*Watts* v. *Spence*, 1976). Even where the contract is completed, if one party has suffered loss through delay in such completion he is entitled to damages (*Raineri* v. *Miles*, 1980).

(c) *Specific performance*

The court nearly always has jurisdiction to award specific performance of a contract for the sale of land though in its discretion, this being an equitable remedy, it may not do so. It will not be granted if there has been unreasonable delay in bringing the action, one party to the contract is under 18 years of age, great hardship would thereby be inflicted on the defendant or the defendant was misled by a substantial mis-statement in the agreement.

Under section 2 of the Chancery Amendment Act 1858 (Lord Cairns's Act):

> "In all cases in which the Court of Chancery has jurisdiction to entertain an application for the specific performance of any covenant, contract, or agreement, it shall be lawful for the same court, if it thinks fit, to award damages to the party injured, either in addition to or in substitution for such specific performance, and such damages may be assessed in such manner as the court shall direct."

Therefore even if the court in its discretion would not award specific performance, it should be able in sales of land to award damages in lieu (*Price* v. *Strange*, 1978).

If a decree of specific performance is not complied with, the injured party can recover damages for breach of contract either at common law or under Lord Cairns's Act (*Johnson* v. *Agnew*, 1979).

(d) *Other remedies*

These include:

(i) Tracing the proceeds of sale in the hands of the vendor (*Lake* v. *Bayliss*, 1974).

(ii) Remedies in tort if there is a conspiracy to induce a breach of contract (*Pritchard* v. *Briggs*, 1979).

(iii) A *Greenwood* v. *Turner* Order. Where the purchaser has taken possession and either a good title has been shown, or the delay in completion is not the vendor's fault or the purchaser performs some act of ownership, the court can order the purchaser to pay the purchase money into court or give up possession.

(iv) Liens: a vendor has an equitable lien on the land for unpaid purchase money, which he may enforce by applying to the court for a resale or for recovery of possession. A purchaser has an equitable lien on the land for the deposit and any expenses incurred pursuant to the contract, which he may enforce by applying to the court for a resale, or, if he tenders the full purchase price, for possession.

(v) A vendor and purchaser summons under section 9 of the Vendor and Purchaser Act 1874, as extended by section 49 (1) and (3) of the Law of Property Act 1925.

(3) Post- completion

After completion a purchaser will generally no longer be able to sue on the contract. Either he will be taken to have waived his rights by proceeding to completion, or the contractual rights will have merged in the conveyance.

Some terms of the contract will be deemed to have survived the conveyance either specifically (*Palmer* v. *Johnson* 1884), or by implication, *e.g. Hisset* v. *Reading Roofing Company*, 1969 (vacant possession to be given on completion). Under The Misrepresentation Act 1967 the remedies of rescission (though unlikely where third parties have acquired rights) and damages survive completion.

Otherwise the purchaser will have to rely on the covenants for title given in the conveyance. These, as explained at p.63, are unsatisfactory.

2. INDEMNITY

This is compensation available from State funds in certain defined circumstances. Under:

(i) The Local Land Charges Act 1975, s. 10 where a person suffers loss arising from the non-registration of a local land charge or from a defective official certificate of search.

(ii) The L.P.A. 1969, s. 25 where a purchaser suffers loss arising from an unknown pre-root registered land charge, provided he comes within the conditions set out in that section.

(iii) The Land Registration Act 1925, s. 83 where the title to land is registered and any person suffers loss because of the rectification or non-rectification of the register, loss or destruction of any deed at the Registry, or an error in the official certificate of search, provided he has not contributed to the loss by fraud or lack of proper care.

Index